PRESENTED BY

Jenny and Dorothy Hill

IN MEMORY OF

Frances Lee Lull

Illustration of Niccolo Paganini by Alison Potter

Nicolo Paganini

This excellent portrait was made in Berlin by Franz Krüger who was a professor at the Academy and Court painter. Many of his portrait drawings were lithographed after his death in 1857 and this one is reproduced by courtesy of the Trustees of the British Museum.

Niccolo Paganini

Supreme Violinist or Devil's Fiddler?

John Sugden

Paganiniana Publications, Inc.
211 West Sylvania Avenue, Neptune City, N.J. 07753

ISBN 0-87666-642-X

Published by PAGANINIANA PUBLICATIONS, INC.
211 West Sylvania Avenue
Neptune City, New Jersey 07753

Contents

Notes on sources

Although bibliographies are usually left to the end of a book, it may be helpful to note here the main origins of the material on which an account of Paganini's life is based, because without this preliminary reference the reader would have to be constantly bothered with footnotes and distracting explanations in the text. A list of books for further reading is added at the end (p. 159).

During his life Paganini himself discussed his youth and earlier career with several people in the full knowledge that these reminiscences would be written up and probably published; some self-justification and romanticizing were therefore inevitable and entirely characteristic. The most often quoted of these biographical sketches was by J. M. Schottky (*Paganini's Leben und Treiben als Kunstler und als Mensch*), first published in Prague in 1830. Since Paganini didn't speak German it's doubtful if he ever read it; but it was used extensively by F. J. Fétis, a well known Belgian critic and music historian who lived mainly in Paris before being appointed Director of the Brussels Conservatoire in 1833. Fétis knew Paganini and had every chance to make notes for a biography but he let the opportunities slip and when he wanted to add the violinist to his great serialised work, *Biographie Universelle des Musiciens*, in 1841, the subject of it was dead. So Fétis had to rely on Schottky, and others, for data and fill in the gaps from his own memory; what he couldn't remember he fabricated and he offended against all modern historical practice by giving full rein to his personal prejudice and bias. In spite of this, Fétis' reputation as a writer was so great that nearly all subsequent biographers of Paganini have used his sketches (he published another one for a Paris musical dictionary in 1851) as their main source, thus perpetuating his mistakes and stories and repeating many of his judgements.

A much more scientific approach to the subject was made nearly a century later by A. Codignola whose book, *Paganini Intimo* (Genoa, 1935), contains two hundred and eighty-seven letters of Paganini, all fully annotated. But it was not until 1957 that a truly comprehensive and scrupulously authenticated biography was produced: *Paganini, the Genoese*, by G. I. C. de Courcy. This massive and scholarly two volume work has at last established the probable truth about a great many contentious episodes in Paganini's life and I am greatly indebted to it.

6

Francois-Joseph Fétis (1784-1871)

Paganini

Acknowledgements

The author and publishers are very grateful to: the University of Oklahoma Press for permission to quote from *Paganini the Genoese* by G. I. C. de Courcy (Copyright 1957); the Mary Evans Picture Library, the British Museum and the British Library, for permission to reproduce a number of illustrations.

The author wishes to express his personal thanks to the following for their generous help in preparing this book:

Jane Sugden, Charles Beare (of Messrs. J. & A. Beare Ltd., London), Andrew McGee, Dr. Giorgio Piumatti (Library of the Conservatario di Musica 'Niccolo Paganini', Genoa), John Ruarke.

Paganini's gold watch and chain. Inside the back cover the following inscription is scratched, possibly by Paganini himself: "il suo caro amico L. G. Germi. N.P."

8

Introduction

There has never been any doubt among musicians that Niccolo Paganini was one of the greatest performers on the violin, or indeed any instrument, who has ever lived. His own music, apart from contemporary accounts of his performances, would be sufficient proof of that. But there has been doubt about his true worth as a musician, as opposed to a technical wizard, and this doubt has never been dispelled.

For many years after his death in 1840 stories continued to be told and written – some of them originating from Paganini himself – about his alleged association with the underworld. Interpretations of this association varied from sordid crimes, such as murder, to a spiritualistic relationship with the devil. Although attempts were made by his friends and associates – and by Paganini himself in his later years – to discount these stories, and although the passage of time has done much to blow away the clouds of superstition, the legend of 'the devil's fiddler' remained a popular one and discredited his reputation to the extent that he was remembered as something of a charlatan and his music was dismissed by critics as nothing more than a trickster's show-box.

This unfair memory has been partly corrected in recent years by two influences: first, the publication of a full length, and fully authenticated, biography in English, which sets the record straight on many inaccuracies and gaps which were repeated in previous biographies; and second, the issue of excellent recordings of some of Paganini's works. It is now possible to evaluate the true musicianship of this remarkable performer and to gauge his influence on the world of music. That is what this book attempts to do.

Inevitably, many details of his life and times have had to be omitted from a book of this length and purpose but it is hoped that enough has been included, in the text and illustrations, to provide a background against which Paganini's extraordinary talents as a musician can be appraised in their true light.

Below: Left: The Vatican Order of the Golden Spur, Grand Cross and miniature, awarded to Paganini by the Pope at the Roman Carnival, 1827.

Below: Right: The Austrian Royal Household medal ("Der Tugend") and miniature, presented to Paganini by the Emperor, 1828.

1 The Prodigy

Genoa is an extraordinary place; a city of ups and downs, of great contrasts between wealth and poverty, beauty and ugliness, order and chaos. It has much in common with the character and life-style of one of its most famous sons – Niccolo Paganini. (The correct Italian spelling is Niccolò or Nicolò.) Genoa rises up from the sea, like one of his own musical themes, in a series of semi-circular terraces, the smooth lines being broken up by buildings of all shapes and sizes which provide endless sets of variations; in the background, the beckoning mountains seem to promise excitement and reward for any who have the courage and skill to cross them and search for fame and fortune in the rich cities of Europe's plains. The child who was born there to Teresa and Antonio Paganini on October 27th, 1782, was destined to cross those mountains and to establish himself as the greatest violinist the world has ever known. But first he had to serve his apprenticeship to a demanding father, a pious mother, an elder brother and three younger sisters, on the seventh floor of a tenement house in a narrow street among those higgledy-piggledy buildings of Genoa.

Antonio Paganini had married Teresa Bocciardo in 1777 and they had six children, of whom Niccolo was the third; the second, another boy, died in infancy. There is no doubt that the family was poor during Niccolo's boyhood; his father's occupation was down in the old port and has been variously described as 'ship's chandler', 'ship's broker', and (in his son's phrase) as a 'not very prosperous tradesman'. But Antonio must have had some enterprise and initiative because during the hard years of the 1790's, when the port of Genoa was blockaded by the British fleet and maritime trade came to a virtual standstill, he was able to make a living as a professional musician and a dealer in mandolins. Niccolo described both his parents as 'musical amateurs' but this was many years later when he had already made his name as a professional; he was never willing to acknowledge much of an artistic debt to his father because he so much resented the memory of being made to work at his violin as a boy. He told Schottky that 'it would be hard to conceive of a stricter father' and even claimed that he was starved of food when Antonio wanted to punish him for insufficient practice. Allowing for some natural exaggeration, it seems likely that these circumstances were basically true: his mother was ambitious for him (she told how an angel had appeared to her in a dream and she had asked that her son might become a great violinist) and his father, once he had recognized the boy's musical ability – a fact which Niccolo *did* acknowledge – had every reason for exploiting it to the full. A general education was in those days regarded as of secondary importance to the development of natural talent. But, more important, the gift of exceptional musical ability to a child in that part of Italy at the end of the eighteenth century was an event which any parent in poor financial circumstances would have welcomed because the potential rewards were so great and so well known.

Northern Italy had been the cradle of nearly all the famous composers of baroque music for strings which formed the nucleus of Court and Church instrumental programmes at the time Niccolo was born. Antonio, as a keen musician, would have been keenly aware of the veneration still accorded to the father of them all, Arcangelo Corelli (born near Milan), to Correlli's pupils Geminiani and Locatelli (born at Lucca and Bergamo respectively), to the great Venetian, Vivaldi, and to that master of Padua – Tartini – to whom students flocked from all over Europe. He can hardly have failed to know about Veracini, the much travelled Florentine, whom some contemporaries considered the world's greatest violinist; and another two – Nardini, born at Leghorn, and Pugnani, born and domiciled in Turin – were still very much alive when Niccolo was a boy. It is inconceivable that in a musical city like Genoa a man of Antonio's interests and shrewdness could have been unaware of the existence of all of these musicians and, particularly, of their envious reputation. He must have seen, in his imagination, the road over the mountains paving the way to his little son's fame and fortune.

'When I was five and a half my father taught me the mandolin', Paganini dictated to a friend, Peter Lichtenthal, who had inconsiderately asked him for an autobiographical sketch at 3 o'clock in the morning. 'At the age of seven I was taught the rudiments of the violin by my father, whose ear was bad although he was passionately fond of music. Within a few months I was able to play any piece of music at sight . . .'. Perhaps this obvious hyperbole is excusable in view of the unseemly hour of the interview. Antonio's lessons evidently included composition as well as violin-teaching: 'Even before I was eight years old', Paganini told Schottky, 'I wrote a sonata under the supervision of my father . . .' The boasts probably contained enough truth to be consistent with the achievements of a musical prodigy because it is proved by the records that Niccolo was giving public performances in Genoa at the age of twelve and he told Schottky that he had played one of his own compositions 'in the big theatre' when he was nine.

Standing in one of the narrow sloping streets of Genoa's old

Birthplace of Paganini in Genoa

Paganini as a boy

town, looking up at the top storey of a tenement house, black with age and neglect, it isn't difficult to imagine Antonio Paganini poring over his calculations for the winning lottery combination (gambling on the lottery was his endless occupation), oblivious of all that went on around him except one thing – Niccolo's practising. If that stopped, or if the boy indulged in too much 'experimenting' with 'new and hitherto unsuspected effects that would astound people' (as Niccolo admitted later), he would scold him and force him back to scales, arpeggios, studies and bowing exercises, the basic technique of a fiddler. Brother, sisters, friends, shouting and screaming while they played in the street below the open windows or clamouring for their mother's attention, had no effect on the ambitious father; it was the grindstone for Niccolo, there was no escape even if he wished for it. But we needn't feel too sorry for him; he had a strong constitution at that time, surviving severe measles at the age of four and scarlet fever at seven; he was probably happy only when he had the little violin tucked under his chin and felt the ease with which bow and fingers responded to every nuance of thought and emotion: exceptionally gifted children are seldom contented unless exercising their special talent.

Niccolo's first professional teacher may have been Giovanni Servetto, a violinist in the theatre orchestra. He never mentioned this name in his reminiscences later and there is only one authority for it, but if his father thought the boy would be content to learn the

Genoa in the early 19th century.

A modern photograph of Genoa with the beckoning hills behind the old town.

routine operatic repertoire from a rank and file fiddler he was mistaken; Niccolo had other ideas and was soon pestering to be taught by a more imaginative professor. It may have been Francesco Gnecco, to whom he went for tuition in composition, who persuaded his father to pay for a six-month course of thirty lessons with his own teacher, Giacomo Costa, the leading violinist in Genoa. 'A very talented boy of twelve, Signor Niccolo Paganini, pupil of the celebrated Signor Giacomo Costa, professor of the violin, played a melodious concerto, which was much admired', said a local newspaper, primly describing a concert of mixed sacred and secular music in one of the Churches given on May 26th, 1795, and we can guess that this 'melodious concerto' was by one of the classical masters on whose music his new teacher had been brought up. Costa was what we should now call 'square', he had little patience with new music and even less with the new technique required to play it; bowing had to be straight up and down – to put it simply – and the kind of bouncing bows and twiddling left-hand plucking which Niccolo loved experimenting with, he frowned upon. But he must have had a sense of humour and the wisdom of a good teacher not to circumscribe his clever pupil too severely because Paganini later referred to him as 'good old Costa' and added – one imagines with a chuckle – that he (Niccolo) 'showed no inclination to adopt his bowing'.

It wasn't merely precocious naughtiness which caused the boy to neglect his professor's advice. At about this time (no certain date is known) he heard August Durand, a young Polish-born emigré to France, who was touring Italy and presumably included Genoa in his itinerary. Durand had perfected the technique of accompanying a tune played with the bow on the upper strings with left-hand pizzicato on the lower ones, and the novelty of this idea, as well as the technical challenge, had a profound effect on Niccolo. It was the beginning of his lasting conception of what violin music should be; it contained the germ of many future compositions and signalled the end of his apprenticeship with the classical composers. We can easily appreciate the difference in style between the baroque and what might be called the new romantic-virtuoso if we compare a violin concerto by Corelli or Vivaldi with one by Paganini; the first primarily requires the performer to have excellent control of rhythm and sustained bowing, the second requires exceptional left-hand dexterity and agility of bowing. These differences will be discussed in a little more detail in a later chapter but meanwhile the slightly condescending epithet of 'good old Costa' which Paganini later used about a man who was only in middle-age when he taught him is understandable. They were stylistically incompatible; one should not blame the professor for failing to develop a pupil whose conception of musical style was basically opposed to his own. As Paganini said later, 'his principles often seemed unnatural to me'.

The six-month course with Costa being completed, where was this eager young prodigy to go next? His father must have asked for advice from musical friends who had some experience of teachers outside Genoa because it was finally decided that he should take the boy to Alessandro Rolla who was leader of the Court Orchestra in Parma, the capital of a duchy over a hundred kilometres to the north east of Genoa, difficult and dangerous of access in those days because of the mountains and the warring French and Austrians. It must have been a major decision for Antonio; he had to leave his wife and family and stake a considerable sum of money on this lad of thirteen who was highly esteemed in Genoa but completely unknown anywhere else. Perhaps no one but a gambler would have been prepared to take the risk. Fortunately, there was a patron,

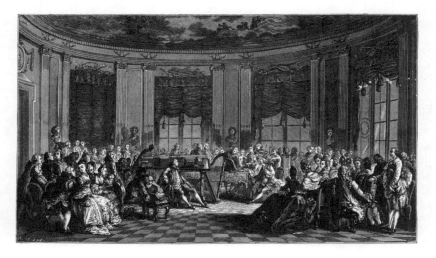

Antonio Paganini must have visualized his son, Niccolo, taking a leading part in court chamber concerts, such as this one in France in the late 18th century.

Marquis Gian Carlo di Negro, who was prepared to help in the true eighteenth century tradition, but it seems that his generosity was insufficient to cover the cost, as the announcement of Niccolo's benefit concert at the theatre makes clear: –

There will be a concert in the Teatro di Sant'Agostino next Friday, July 31. It will be given by Niccolo Paganini of Genoa, a boy already known in his native city for his skill as a violinist. Having decided to go to Parma to perfect himself in his profession under the guidance of the renowned Professor Rolla, and not being in a position to defray the many necessary expenses, he has conceived this plan to give him courage to ask his fellow citizens to contribute towards his project, hereby inviting them to be present at this event which he hopes will prove enjoyable.

The results of this concert – and there may have been others – in terms of money are unknown but in September, 1795, father and son set out on their great adventure, possibly accompanied at least part of the way by di Negro. On arrival in Parma, Antonio and Niccolo presented themselves and their letters of introduction to Professor Rolla, whom they discovered ill in bed. Asked by his wife to wait in an ante-room, they found a violin lying on the table together with Rolla's latest concerto (presumably still in manuscript). 'On a sign from my father', as Niccolo told Schottky, 'I took up the violin and played the composition off at sight'. This

Parma, where Antonio and Niccolo sought out Prof. Rolla in 1795.
(Reproduced by kind permission of the Parma Commune).

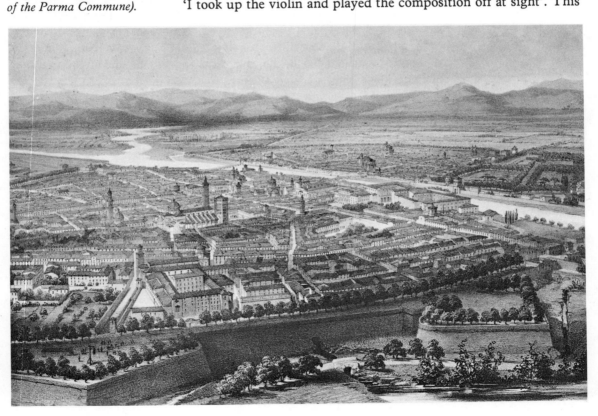

well known story probably contains two grains of truth, the father's opportunism and the son's precocious talent. According to Niccolo, Rolla couldn't believe at first that it was only a little boy playing but having satisfied himself on that point, he said, 'I also can teach you nothing'. (He must have read Costa's letter by this time.) 'For goodness sake go to Paër! Here you'd only be wasting your time.'

So off they went, probably a bit dejected, to see Ferdinando Paër, a native of Parma who was Director of the Conservatory there and a composer of operas. Niccolo seems to have made a good impression on him because, although he couldn't take him as his pupil straight away and passed him on to his own teacher – Gasparo Ghiretti – he became interested in him later and they worked closely together on composition for several months. When Paër went to Vienna to compose a work for the Italian Opera there, Niccolo says, 'We parted for a long time. But later I always returned with delight to this great master and am happy to call myself his grateful pupil'. Such an accolade from one who was not usually so generous in his acknowledgement of other people's talents, would indicate that Paër's ability as a teacher exceeded his achievement as a composer, since after the advent of Rossini his works passed into oblivion where they have remained. He must also have been a man of fickle loyalty because having been a protégé of Napoleon (the French captured Parma in the year after the Paganinis arrived) and having composed the bridal march for the Emperor's wedding to Josephine in 1810, he later became a royalist and was appointed director of the King's chamber music in 1832. He was much disliked by other professional musicians, being regarded as egotistic, self-interested, and consumed by jealousy. The fact that Niccolo got on with him so well is not, therefore, a good testimonial to his own character. But the strong theatrical bias in Paër's experience may well have made a lasting impression on Paganini and may account for the dramatic nature of many of his later compositions.

Another influence which affected him at this time was a strange solo violin work by Pietro Locatelli called *L'arte di nuova modulazione* and sub-titled *Capricci Enigmatici,* published some sixty years earlier but ignored – if they had ever heard of it – by professors of the classical style. Niccolo implied to Fétis that he came across the work by accident and if so he certainly must have been excited by it because these Locatelli caprices contained all the effects which he himself was experimenting with and endeavouring to write down in a way which could be expressed by accepted musical notation. The question of whether these technical feats, sometimes referred to derogatively as the 'tricks of modern finger-heroes', were the only rungs of the ladder which Paganini climbed and on which his reputation as a performer-composer should be judged, is an important one and will be discussed later; the point to

17

note now is that at the early age of 14 or 15 he was unwilling to follow the classical masters slavishly, even as they were taught by respected professors like Paër, because his musical nature hankered after a style which was totally different. If his father had removed him from Genoa to Parma in order to ensure that he was educated to follow in the hallowed footsteps of the classical masters, he must have been disappointed; in this very impressionable period of his musical life, Niccolo became bent on treading a very different path.

The expedition to Parma seems to have done nothing to bring parent and son closer together at any level. Niccolo told Schottky that his father's 'extreme severity' seemed to him more oppressive than ever. 'I should like to have broken away from him so that I might have travelled alone,' he continued, 'but my severe mentor never left my side and accompanied me through most of the towns of northern Italy ... where I gave concerts and received great applause.' The latter part of this reminiscence may have been a figment of the imagination because as soon as the French invaded northern Italy in March, 1796, it's likely that Antonio would have wanted to return immediately to the rest of his family rather than to risk an extensive tour through the heart of the battlefield with a young boy. Even Genoa shortly became too hot with revolutionary fervour for comfort, so the Paganinis packed up and went to their country property at Ramairone where, according to Niccolo's memory about thirty years later, he dedicated himself to agriculture and amused himself by twanging the guitar. The family must have had a small holding in this remote and peaceful valley and no doubt the boys were encouraged to lend a hand with the cultivation of vegetables and fruit; all food was in very short supply because of the British naval blockade of the ports. However, it seems that at the turn of the century Antonio was able to resume his maritime work because he and Niccolo spent a long time at Leghorn, away from the family, during which the boy gave occasional concerts and continued his experiments in composition.

If these occupations sound rather desultory after the excitements of Parma and the early promise of the young prodigy, one must remember the disruption and confusion caused in this part of the country by the war. The French army which General Bonaparte led along the coast-road from Nice to Genoa in 1796 was very different from the one with which the First Consul shattered the Austrians at Marengo four years later. In '96 he had told his half-starved and ragged soldiers: 'I am about to lead you into the most fertile plains in the world; fruitful provinces and large cities will soon lie at your mercy; there you will find honour, profit, and wealth'. He was right; the soldiers did find wealth in these 'fruitful provinces' at the expense of many helpless Italian families, whether they were rich or relatively poor, like the Paganinis. It was of little help for some

18

towns and cities to welcome the French as liberators, to fly the tricolour – as the Genoese did – in an effort to proclaim their identity with republican principles; all conquered cities are alike to hungry and rapacious soldiers, they are ripe for pillage whether their inhabitants sympathise with the invaders' political aims or not. None of the main combatants had much sympathy to spare for the native population; Nelson himself described Naples and Sicily as being made up of 'fiddlers, poets, harlots, and scoundrels'. The same sort of contempt was shared by the French and Austrians for the civilian population in the north and it must have required no little ingenuity and enterprise on the part of Antonio to keep a humble family like the Paganinis, who fitted at least one aspect of Nelson's description, intact. Perhaps cultivating vegetables and twanging the guitar were the safest occupations for Niccolo during these troubled times.

But there is evidence that the high-spirited youth was far from content to allow these years between boyhood and manhood to waste away. The romantic episode which Fétis used to fill up this sketchily documented period, in which Niccolo is supposed to have 'retired to the country estate in Tuscany of a lady of rank' who revived his interest in the guitar and was the 'Signora Dida' in the dedication of various minor works thought to have been composed at this time, is almost certainly fictitious. Much more likely is De Courcy's conjecture that father and son led a difficult and disrupted life, journeying between Leghorn and Ramairone, with Niccolo pestering to be allowed off on his own and occasionally succeeding for the odd night or two, with the excuse of a concert here and there. What is certain is that at last, in September 1801, at the age of eighteen, he was allowed to attend the festival at Lucca,

"... large cities will soon lie at your mercy . . ." Napoleon's words were soon put into action by the French armies in N. Italy and Venice was no exception, as this print of the looting of the golden horses of St. Mark's shows. It happens to be very topical, since the Italians have recently removed three of the four horses themselves, to save them, this time, from damage by pollution.

19

accompanied by his elder brother, to compete for the honour of performing in the Cathedral during the religious celebrations. According to his own account (to Peter Lichtenthal) he swept all the other competitors off the board and when he repeated the performance in the evening it was received with great applause, although a member of the Cathedral orchestra at the time said that he was unwise enough to play a piece which imitated bird-songs and other musical instruments, which aroused laughter. One can imagine this was not popular with the ecclesiastical dignitaries but it evidently pleased the young, especially those who welcomed Niccolo as a Jacobin because he hailed from the revolutionary port of Genoa. His reception in Lucca was so encouraging that he decided to make a final bid for freedom by sending word back home

This 19th century print of Lucca, with the cathedral tower in the background, gives an idea of its old-fashioned peace and quiet – an atmosphere which it has to some extent retained up to the present – see opposite.

20

with his brother that he was staying on there; Antonio no doubt received the news with mixed anxiety, resignation and relief, like most parents who are presented with a unilateral declaration of freedom by a rebellious offspring.

The annual festivities at Lucca ended in December and soon afterwards Niccolo was appointed 'first violin of the Republic' of Lucca indicating that he had won recognition not only of his musical prowess but of his political principles also. Not that the latter meant anything to him, he was much more interested in the

pretty girls, the gambling at the Baths, the music-making and the genial friendship of this cultured little town. He scraped up just enough money to keep himself by teaching and by giving concerts in neighbouring towns; in the true romantic tradition of impoverished artists (Lucca was the birthplace of the composer of *La Bohéme*) he was rich one day, having won at the tables, and broke the next. As he confessed to Schottky, 'I often fell into the hands of people who played (i.e. gambled) with more finish and success than I (and) often lost in one evening the fruit of several concerts, finding myself in difficulties from which only my art was able to extricate me'.

That he had the luck of the gambler, as well as the occasional misfortune, is shown by the story of his 'winning' two superb violins at this time. He told Schottky that while on a 'pleasure visit' to Leghorn he was asked to give a concert but had no instrument to play on, so a wealthy business man (M. Livron) lent him a Guarneri for the occasion and was so impressed with Niccolo's performance that he refused to take it back at the end. 'Keep the instrument, dear Paganini', Livron is reported to have said, 'and look upon it as a souvenir'. On a later occasion, this time in Parma, a Signor Pasini challenged him to play a very difficult piece at sight, promising him a valuable violin (another Guarneri) if he succeeded. 'I won it', Niccolo recalled, without giving any further details of the test. [*]

Apart from these few recollections, Niccolo was very reticent about the first three years he spent as a free-lance in Lucca. This is not surprising; the war and all the revolutionary excitement stirred up by the French invasion made regular travel impossible, so he was unable, yet, to launch himself as an itinerant virtuoso, although he obviously had all the talent and all the confidence required to do so. Again, it's not surprising that he was reluctant to delve too deep into his memory of the extra-musical activities of these years; a young man just released from strict parental control, endowed with Paganini's ardent temperament and hot Genoese blood, enjoys a life which he is not anxious to reveal in every detail nearly thirty years later when he is trying to present himself to the world as a mature concert-artist of comparative respectability. Finally, Paganini's own explanation of this reticence to Schottky, couched as it is in the language of evasion, probably contains at least a measure of truth:

If it were a habit of mine to keep a diary, if I collected press notices . . . or if I carried about with me only a fraction of the numerous letters I have received from more or less good friends, I should be able to tell you endless anecdotes of my youth and career . . . But how is it possible at present to collect my thoughts so as to reply adequately . . . to the most necessary questions of a biographer?

---

[*]Full details of the instruments in Paganini's possession at the time of his death, and their subsequent history, are given in Appendix V of De Courcy (*Op. cit.*).

Semi-caricature sketch of Paganini

Caricature demonstrating Paganini's unique bowing technique

It may have been as convenient for Paganini not to be able to remember too much about the days of sowing his wild oats in Lucca and its environs as it must have been frustrating for Schottky not to be able to fill in the biographical details. Later on, the less savoury episodes in his private life became public property because he was a celebrity; perhaps it is better that the earlier escapades should remain shrouded in mystery, in spite of subsequent attempts – some benevolent, some malicious, and others simply inept – to paint the whole picture from imagination.

What is unfortunate is Schottky's failure to elicit from Paganini any information about his compositions at this time or about his re-appointment in Lucca after the arrival there of Napoleon's sister, Princess Elise. By inference, his first three Opus numbers are attributed to this period but as the Opus I contains the best music he ever wrote (*Twenty Four Caprices for solo violin*) one would like to know more about its sources of inspiration and the occasions on which he performed the Caprices publicly, if he ever did. Chronologically, we know that he returned to Genoa briefly at the end of 1804, presumably to escape the epidemic of yellow fever which was then decimating Leghorn and the surrounding area, but had returned to Lucca by January of the following year. A few months later Napoleon crowned himself king of Italy in Milan and shortly afterwards farmed out some of the principalities to members of his family; to Elise and her husband, Felix Baciocchi, he gave the states of Piombino and Lucca. Thus, the little town which had previously been an independent Republic now became the seat of government for a young woman of twenty-eight who, like her famous brother, had strong views about the regulation of her subjects' behaviour and was already renowned for her proud bearing and haughty manner. More immediately important for Niccolo, however, was the fact that she was a patroness of the arts and was certain to establish a court orchestra; moreover, her husband was a keen amateur violinist (Napoleon described the hobby as his 'worst eccentricity') and would certainly require a teacher. Niccolo had inherited his father's opportunism and he was already acknowledged to be the leading violinist and the most outstanding musician in Lucca, so perhaps it's not surprising that instead of continuing his promising career as a free-lance travelling virtuoso he hung about in the town where he had so many friends and pleasures, waiting for the moment when the new Princess would summon him to her court and offer him a lucrative appointment as her Master of Music. Unfortunately for him, things didn't turn out quite as he expected.

2 Court–Musician and Composer

With typical Bonaparte efficiency, Princess Elise recruited her new court orchestra at Lucca from among the many musicians previously employed by the old Cappella and the relatively modern Republic, pensioning off the old lags and reducing its size to that of a chamber group. In such circumstances of stringent economy, Niccolo and his brother may perhaps have considered themselves lucky to be taken on since they had been previously employed for only three years. But it can't have pleased Niccolo much to discover that Giuseppe Romaggi, who had twenty-seven years' service, was appointed first violin while he had to take over the second, at what he called 'a piffling little salary' of only just over 1,000 francs a year – much less than he could have earned as a free-lance. Of course, in addition to this he was paid for the lessons he gave to Prince Felix and for special performances outside the normal court routine. There can't have been much time for free-lance engagements while the Court was in residence because Elise kept her musicians busy: 'I had to conduct each time the royal family went to the opera', he told Schottky, 'play three times a week at court, and every fortnight give a big concert at the formal soirées . . .' But the frequent absences of the Princess – she had several country houses, including the palace at Massa where she ordered the Cathedral to be demolished because it spoilt the view – must have given him time to compose and to indulge his 'youthful foibles' which were particularly prevalent at this time (he admitted to Schottky that 'as a youth I was by no means free from the errors of young people, who, after the upbringing of a slave, are suddenly freed from their bonds and seek to reward themselves for long privation by heaping pleasure upon pleasure').

Exactly when, for how long, and to what extent he shared some of these pleasures with the Princess herself are debatable points; possibly their relationship never developed into any kind of intimacy. The morals of the court were said to be lax but Elise was such a haughty Princess that it seems unlikely she would have demeaned herself to the extent of risking a liaison with so humble a subject as one of her musicians. On the other hand, he told Lichtenthal that 'she sometimes swooned when hearing me play' and to Schottky he hinted broadly that there was sufficient intimacy between them to cause her to leave the concerts early 'because my

24

music placed too great a strain on her nerves'. We know that he made eyes at a large number of ladies at court while he played but whether it was the music or the ogleing which caused distress to the Princess, or neither, we shall never know; with Paganini, as with some writers of fiction, it's impossible to tell how much he believed in his own stories. The enigmatic smile which no doubt accompanied his recollections to his friends in later life was already well practised by the time he was twenty-five.

That his mind was divided during these years as a court-musician between serious work and light-hearted musical entertainments of an amorous nature is clearly indicated by the compositions he is known to have written. He told Schottky how one day he promised 'another charming lady' a surprise at the next concert – 'a little musical prank having reference to our relationship'. This turned out to be a piece played only on the top and bottom strings of the violin (the E and G) depicting a dialogue between lovers, the ten movements being suitably entitled (i.e. Flirtation, Request, Consent, Timidity, Gratification, Quarrel, Reconciliation, etc.). He recollected that this 'amusing novelty' went down very well with

An early portrait of Paganini
– probably dated 1813.

25

the lady for whom it was intended and was received by the court with great applause. The Princess, either because she was the lady in question or because she was deceived by the composer, overwhelmed him with compliments on this performance and asked him – in a parody of Queen Victoria's remark to Sir Arthur Sullivan after hearing one of his light operas – 'Now that you have already played something so beautiful on two strings, couldn't you let us hear something on one string?' The idea appealed to Niccolo and he at once set about composing a piece for the G string alone which he entitled *Napoleon Sonata* and performed on the Emperor's birthday which occurred a few weeks later, again to great applause. 'This was the beginning and the real origin', he remembered, 'of my fancy for the G string. Later, people always wanted to hear more works of this kind and so I progressed from day to day until finally I had completely mastered this style of playing'.

The fact that Paganini took the trouble to write out these novelties in full (they were found among his autographed collection after his death) indicates that he took them more seriously than his memory of their first performance might convey. Indeed, their original titles – *Duetto Amoroso* for violin and guitar, and *Prima Sonata con Variazione per la 4ta corda* – provide a clue that they may not have been quite the spontaneous compositions that he wanted his biographers to believe. But it's certainly true that the *Napoleon Sonata* was the first of several works he wrote for the G string alone and played with success on his later concert tours.

This brings us to consider for the first time whether Paganini deserves to be judged as a serious composer for the violin or whether his works for the instrument should be classified as little more than a trickster's show-box. It's true that works like the *Love Duet*, or the *Duo Merveille*, which were written at about the same time and dedicated to Princess Elise, show nothing more than an exceptional technique; their musical value is negligible. But another work which is credited to this period, although it may have been written over a number of years, is the Opus I *Twenty-four Caprices for solo violin*, and here we have something of an entirely different calibre. If Paganini had composed nothing for the violin except these Caprices he would have earned a place alongside J. S. Bach as one of the great benefactors of the violinist's repertoire; he would also have saved himself, incidentally, a lot of posthumous criticism. The Caprices contain music to be cherished by violinists, and by audiences, for their originality, great variety, and unsophisticated beauty. Proof of this has been provided by Liszt, Schumann, Brahms and Rachmaninov, who, among others, made adaptations from them. They are so difficult in their original form that public performances are rare events but anyone who has not heard or studied them will be repaid by acquiring a recording (see

The first page of Paganini's 24th Caprice in A minor, from the 1st Edition published by Ricordi of Milan in 1820.
©G. Ricordi & Co. (London) Ltd. – reproduced by permission.

Discography, p. 162). To take one Caprice as an example, that in E major, No. 9: here we have a taste of Paganini's imitation technique, the player being instructed to play the first seven and a half bars to sound as much like two flutes as possible (*imitando i Flauti*). Not only has the player to cope with double-stopping (i.e. playing on the top two strings simultaneously) but is instructed also to bow softly, sweetly, and gently (*sulla tastiera*—close to the fingerboard). This 'flute' phrase is immediately complemented by four bars to be played loudly and emphatically in imitation of two horns (*imitando i Corni*) on the bottom two strings. These opening bars form the basis of the whole Caprice, though the added material (in different keys) provides plenty of variety—bouncing bows, harmonics, octaves, and runs in the highest register of the instrument—many of the 'tricks', in fact, which were so characteristic of the composer. But the effect is musical, not merely showy; from beginning to end, this piece has structure, rhythm, melody, and style. In musical terms, it has meaning. Most of the Caprices are similarly endowed, there is scarcely one which is merely an exercise in technical dexterity. Thus we can state categorically that anyone who condemns Paganini as a composer on the grounds of mere showsmanship cannot have studied the *Twenty-four Caprices* and although some of his later works fail to live up to their standard, he should be judged, as a composer, by them. The dedication (*Agli artisti*—'To the artists') indicates that Paganini himself would have wished it.

The *Twenty-four Caprices* were published by G. Riccordi of Milan in 1820, and together with Op. 2, 3, 4 and 5, were the only works which Paganini published during his lifetime.* The other works are minor compared with the Caprices: Op. 2 and 3 are two sets of six Sonatas for violin and guitar, the second set being dedicated to Eleonora Quilici, a dress-maker and youngest daughter of a family of musicians with whom Niccolo was on very friendly terms (his genuine and unsullied affection for Eleonora is attested by his financial support of her during the rest of his life and by the bequest in his will of an annual pension of 600 lire for life; she was the only beneficiary in his will outside his close family). Op. 4 and 5 are two sets of three quartets for violin, viola, 'cello and guitar, reflecting the composer's close attention to chamber music during these years at Lucca; the dedication of both sets 'to the admirers of Niccolo Paganini' indicates that they were written for the unassuming friends with whom he played them, most likely members of the Quilici family.

---

*Full details of Paganini's compositions are given in De Courcy (*Op. Cit.*) Appx. IV, with the exception of the Concerto in E minor (No. 6 Op. Posth.) which has been discovered since her book was published.

Thus we can imagine Niccolo leading a double life at Lucca after the pompous arrival of Princess Elise. On the one hand, he filled the rôle of the courtier, paying lip-service to the strict etiquette laid down by his royal mistress while enjoying the flirtations which she and her ladies encouraged; on the other hand, he pursued a private life which was part serious – including composition and practice – and part frivolous, including the gaming tables and more

Princess Elise Baciocchi, sister of Napoleon I, Duchess of Piombino and Lucca, later Grand Duchess of Tuscany. Paganini was appointed to her court at Lucca, as a member of the orchestra (2nd desk), in 1805. This portrait of her by Stefan Tofanelli is considered by some opinions to have been flattering but as he held the post of court painter this would not be surprising.

29

ephemeral love-making. One can understand that such a life in the comparative security of pleasant Lucca, while other parts of Italy were still in political turmoil, might have satisfied a young man in his late twenties, if ambition had played no part in his plans. But Niccolo was ambitious and an event which occurred late in 1807 must have convinced him that in attaching himself to the mercurial whims of Princess Elise he was backing a loser. The State Archives of Lucca reveal that in November of that year the Princess dissolved her orchestra, retaining only a string quartet (which included Niccolo and his brother, each on the same salary), a singer, and a *maestro di cappella*. This must have been a shattering blow to his ambition and pride: no orchestra to accompany him, no distinction between him and his much less talented brother, no prospect of future promotion. His immediate reaction was to apply for two months' leave of absence and to go home to Genoa, presumably to discuss the situation with his family. He also took the opportunity to give two concerts in Turin where Felice Blangini was Court musician, and lover, to Elise's sister Pauline (Princess Borghese); Blangini heard him play on these occasions and on his return to Paris told Fétis about this 'wonderful new star', thus promoting Paganini's talent beyond the Alps for the first time. The legendary story that Niccolo himself accomplished a whirlwind love-affair with Princess Pauline while he was in Turin is demolished by de Courcy (*Op. Cit.* I 104-6) with characteristic efficiency.

In fact Niccolo was back in Lucca for the summer of 1808, giving a concert at the beautiful Villa Marlia, one of Elise's homes just outside the town, on August 8th. But although he remained on good terms with Prince Felix, being employed as his teacher and quartet-leader, his association with the Princess was nearly over. She had at last persuaded her brother to give her a more important territory to rule, becoming Grand Duchess of Tuscany with her court at Florence in March, 1809. Her stupendous conceit and overbearing manner were naturally enlarged to an even greater extent by this aggrandizement, so it's quite likely that the story told by one of Paganini's earliest biographers (Conestabile) about the final break may be true. According to that, Niccolo appeared at a gala function at court in the uniform of a captain of the guards, presumably as a joke or as a deliberate provocation, being aware of the Princess' sensitivity on such matters. She ordered him to change into black court dress but he refused and paraded through the ballroom in his uniform, no doubt revelling in the attention he was drawing to himself. Later that night, however, he realised he had overdone the buffoonery and departed from court for good, refusing to return in spite of the Princess' rather too pressing offers to forgive. This story, if true, would account for the suddenness of

Scenes of Florence: the Battistero (above) and Ponte Vecchio (below)

Franz Joseph Haydn (1732-1809), Austrian composer

Typical orchestra of the late eighteenth century

his departure from Florence at the end of the year 1809 but the real cause of his self-emancipation from the fetters of a paid servant at court lay much deeper and to understand this we must take a look at the employment situation for musicians in Europe at this time.

When Joseph Haydn was asked towards the end of his life why he had never written any quintets, (bearing in mind his many works for other combinations of players), he is said to have replied: 'Because nobody ordered any'. This classic reply sums up better than any long history the motivation for a court-composer in the eighteenth century. Music to order, or 'occasional music' as it is sometimes called, was performed once and then put away in a drawer and forgotten – or, rather, it was forgotten by most people but sometimes remembered by the composer who re-used a particularly good tune in a later work. The quality and style of such music depended as much on the patron as on the composer; if Princess Elise had been a really discerning woman with anything like a serious musical background, we should almost certainly have had much more from Paganini's pen of the calibre of the *Twenty four Caprices* instead of trivial stuff like the *Duetto Amoroso*. The way an artist developed owed much to the demands made on him by the employer and Niccolo may have been unfortunate at such a formative period in his life to be employed by a woman whose musical taste was immature and superficial. Although there appears to be no record of any expression of frustration by him with the poor standard of music at the Baciocchi court, strong evidence is provided in two letters written by a friend of Prince Felix (quoted by De Courcy, *Op. Cit.* I 108-9), a regular visitor who took part in the 'bad quartets' which followed the 'royal dinners'. The writer (Boucher de Perthes, who later achieved renown as an archaeologist) is clearly referring to the private quartets held in the Prince's own residence rather than to the music played at the Princess' court but the references to Niccolo's 'clowning', and the fact that these references evidently made the Grand Duchess laugh, tell us enough about the level of music-making at the courts of Lucca and Florence to guess at what depths it had reached. There can surely be no doubt that in his more reflective and serious moments Paganini rejected these standards as beneath contempt; no true musician could have tolerated them for long and it is much more likely that he fled from the Tuscan court for artistic reasons than for disciplinary ones.

Another factor which contributed to this was the size of the orchestra at Lucca. As we have seen, Princess Elise reduced her chamber orchestra to a string quartet at the end of 1807. Haydn's permanent chamber orchestra at Esterhaza in 1783 consisted of eleven violins, two violas, two 'cellos, two double-basses, two oboes, two bassoons, and two horns; other instruments were added when the music demanded them.* Many of the European courts at the end of the eighteenth century also maintained an opera-house, with its full complement of instrumental players, to which the local citizens were admitted free of charge. Although such luxury had but a short time to live (it was greatly reduced by the cost of the Napoleonic wars), the comparison between the circumstances in which Niccolo found himself at Lucca and Florence and those which pertained elsewhere, particularly in Germany, is one which must have struck him forcibly, if he realised it. By the time he was engaged again in court-music (at Parma in 1836) he had experienced the great superiority of the German orchestras to the Italian but at the time we are discussing he was probably unaware of comparative standards elsewhere, otherwise he could never have endured the music at the Baciocchi court for as long as three years.

Finally, the relationship between Niccolo and his patrons (Princess Elise and her husband) seems to have been much less formal than was usual at other European courts of comparative size and importance. At Brunswick, for example, Spohr had to put up with the kind of insensitive treatment which a musician with Paganini's temperament might not have been able to tolerate. Spohr describes in his autobiography how he and his colleagues had to suffer when the Duke was not present:

The Court concerts in the apartments of the Duchess took place once a week and were most disagreeable to the musicians of the ducal orchestra, for according to the prevailing custom cards were played during the music. In order not to be disturbed the Duchess had ordered the orchestra always to play *piano*. The leader, therefore, left out the trumpets and kettle drums and instructed strangers that no *forte* should be played in its full strength. As this was not always to be avoided in symphonies however softly the band might play the Duchess ordered a thick carpet to be spread out under the orchestra in order to deaden sound . . . One day when the Duke was not there and for that reason nobody was listening to the music, the prohibition regarding the 'f' being renewed and the dreadful carpet again spread, I tried a new concerto of my own. I can only call these performances rehearsals because no preparation was ever made before-hand excepting for those at which we knew the Duke would be present. Engrossed with my work which I heard for the first time with the orchestra I quite forgot the prohibition and played with all the vigour and fire of inspiration so that I even carried away the orchestra with me. Suddenly in the middle of the solo my arm was seized by a lackey who whispered to me 'Her Highness sends me to tell you that you are not to scrape away so feverishly'. Enraged at this interruption I played if possible yet more loudly and so afterwards was obliged to put up with a rebuke from the Marshall of the Court.

With all her insufferable airs and graces, Princess Elise doesn't

---

A Social History of Music by Henry Raynor. (London, 1972) p 306.

seem to have subjected Niccolo to that degree of humiliation, although he told George Harrys (later his secretary-manager) that he 'had to suffer many a vexation' while he was in her service. He was referring to the need to obtain permission from the court officials if he wanted to be absent for any length of time, or if he wanted to hold a private party; but he must have known that this was the usual custom and no court-musician, however much in favour, could expect freedom of action. It was a matter of choice: either the security of regular employment with the drudgery of music to order, or the freedom of independence with the risk of no work. The circumstances are different in our age but the basic situation hasn't changed much.

If Paganini had been luckier in the artistic standards demanded at Lucca and later at Florence, he might possibly have settled there for some years and established his name as a great teacher as well as a great performer, in the tradition of his Florentine predecessor, Nardini, who made such a strong impression on Dr. Burney when he met and heard him during his visit in 1770. But Niccolo chose freedom and in the light of the evidence we can't blame him.

The year 1809 was thus the watershed in his life, the turning point when he decided to make his living as a free-lance soloist

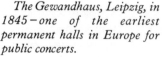

The Gewandhaus, Leipzig, in 1845 – one of the earliest permanent halls in Europe for public concerts.

performing his own music, instead of pursuing the traditional occupation of a court-musician who founded his own school of violinists. In terms of money he had no cause to regret the decision after about 1820 but in terms of mental and physical health he may have had. It might be argued that a temperament like his required the constant stimulus of concert-giving, the excitement of applause, the restlessness of travel. It could also be said that the new concert-going public needed a bizarre personality like his to put over the extravagant type of music he was already composing. To form a conclusion on these matters we will now consider the musical world which Niccolo was about to enter and the face he prepared to show it.

The origin of the regular public concert has been traced to Germany in the mid-eighteenth century. In Leipzig, for example, a series of subscription concerts had been organised by a society of amateur performers for some years before a permanent hall (the 'Gewandhaus') was found for them by the municipal authorities in 1781. Five years later the professional players of the State Theatre asked to be amalgamated with the society and thus was formed an orchestra which was to become famous under Mendelssohn in the next century and remains so to-day. In other German towns and cities small concert-societies sprang up, with amateur performers and financial backing from public subscriptions but it was a risky venture for even a well known and respected professional musician to put on a concert under such auspices; audiences made up from bourgeois music-lovers were an unknown quantity and the financial rewards, as well as the artistic standards, were impossible to predict. Shortly after Mozart had established himself in Vienna, having at last escaped from the dreadful patronage of the Archbishop of Salzburg, he risked association with just such a body in order to have some of his instrumental works performed but unfortunately no record exists to tell us the results.* Later on he ran his own subscription concerts but even his growing fame as an opera-composer couldn't turn these into a success.** Beethoven, refusing to be tied to the routine of subscription concerts, persuaded his rich friends to sponsor public concerts of his works until a new Viennese society (the *Gesellschaft der Musikfreunde*) took on the patronage in 1813.*** In the same year in London the 'Philharmonic Society' was founded, one of the original 30 members being Charles Neate who claimed to be Beethoven's only English pupil. This was composed of gifted amateurs who promoted, and performed in, eight concerts a season at the Argyll

---

*See his letter of 8 May, 1782, in *The Letters of Mozart and his family*, Tr. by Emily Anderson. (London, 1938).
**See Henry Raynor, *Op. Cit.* p 324.
****Ibid.* p 329.

Rooms, Regent Street, and, as the preliminary announcement makes clear, the purpose was to fill the gap in the public performance of instrumental music in the capital, which had fallen into 'almost utter neglect'. The record of the first century of the Society's activities (*History of the Philharmonic Society of London* by M. B. Foster, London, 1912) makes interesting reading because it reveals a wealth of information about commissioned works, the dates of first performances, and the names of conductors and soloists, many of whom became famous but who were then relatively unknown. For example, the first performance of a Paganini work (the B minor Concerto) at one of the Society's concerts was in April 1844, so that in spite of his triumphant début in London thirteen years earlier he was not thought of highly enough to be invited by the Society as a guest soloist on subsequent visits. In France and Italy the orchestral public concert had almost as long a history as in Germany but it was not until the early nineteenth century that a regular audience was built up in a few of the leading towns.

Enough has been said to indicate that when Niccolo decided to launch himself as a free-lance soloist the public concert was still in its infancy and there was no guarantee that even a well known virtuoso would be successful. Apart from the difficulties of

The interior of the Hanover Square Concert Room, London, in 1843 – this was one of the earliest public concert halls in England.

obtaining a hall and an orchestral accompaniment of a reasonable standard, there was the problem of promotion and, for a new composer, the fear that *un*familiarity would breed contempt. In Italy, where his name was not yet generally known, the opera-house was the only venue where a new star had a good chance of being appreciated; opera was the rage and the more theatrical the performance, the more likely the public approbation. Niccolo was attracted to the theatre for two obvious reasons: it fulfilled his need to escape from the world of harsh realities – a common enough reason but a pressing one for a person of Niccolo's fervent character and temperament – and secondly, actresses in Italian provincial theatres were sometimes pretty and usually of easy virtue. When he was on concert tours in later life he always made straight for the theatre, however tired he might be, as soon as he arrived in a town, in the hope of gratifying both necessities. Such an inveterate frequenter of the pit and the stage-door could hardly fail to acquire some of their theatricalism, which he loved so much and it is reasonable to assume that when he considered his own public image, which he was now forced to do, the stage figured as prominently in his mind as the concert-platform. In fact, for most of his public concert career, which was just beginning, he performed on many more stages than platforms, often as an 'intermezzo', sandwiched between the acts of a play, an opera,

The elegant portrait by J. A. D. Ingres, dated 1818, showing Paganini in a flattering light. It was executed in Rome where the artist was then struggling to make a living with his pencil-drawings of visitors to the city.

36

The portrait by George Patten of 1832, when Paganini was about 50. The original painting belongs to Messrs. W. E. Hill & Sons, Great Missenden, by whose permission it is reproduced here, and who also possess Paganini's letter to the artist expressing his appreciation of the portrait.

or a ballet. Against such a backing, it would have been uncommercial – as well as untypical – for so imaginative an artist not to present himself in a dramatic style. In what rôle did he decide during the next three years to cast himself?

The portrait by Ingres, of 1819, shows him as a rather debonnair figure, a pleasant smile playing on his unlined features, the deeply sunken eyes quietly confident, the violin tucked comfortably under his right arm and the bow held elegantly by fingers which peep out of a sleeve which is a shade too long. His hair curls naturally on a high forehead and has not yet been allowed to grow long: altogether a most respectable and rather imposing personality. Was that the real Paganini of this time? One feature is certainly missing from the Ingres portrait – his buffoonery. Boucher de Perthes, quoted earlier, wrote to his father from Leghorn in 1810: –

I've told you of an Italian with whom I made music at Prince Baciocchi's. He's just been giving some concerts here which have been a great success. He's a Genoese by the name of Paganini and is self-taught; therefore, he plays like nobody else. But he spoils his playing by buffooneries unworthy of the art and his fine talent. I've heard him add a cadenza to a concerto of Viotti's in which he imitates a donkey, a dog, a rooster, etc. . . . .

37

Fétis (quoting an earlier source) tells of a similar piece of pantomime at a concert in Ferrara (referred to in the next Chapter) where Niccolo imitated a donkey, and de Courcy (*Op. Cit.* I, p. 113) quotes a local reviewer who wrote that after a string had broken, 'he went right on playing as though nothing had happened, imitating perfectly on the remaining three a dog, a cat, a nightingale, a cock and hen'.

It seems, then, that one rôle Niccolo was determined to display to the public was that of the comedian. To Italian audiences in small towns in the north, this was clearly acceptable. De Perthes wrote (in the same letter): —

The Italians – who love these 'tours de force' – applaud him like mad and, when he leaves the theatre, three hundred people follow him to his hotel.

But if the comic side of his personality was never far below the surface, there was also a much darker aspect which may have already begun to emerge during these early years of his public career and which later made such a deep impression on audiences. This aspect concerns his reputed association with the world of sorcery and witchcraft. The portrait attributed to George Patten, of 1833, when Paganini was 50, shows a very different image from the Ingres. In the later portrait, the eyes have assumed an air of mystery, the expression is sardonic, the long dark hair and side-whiskers frame sunken cheeks and aquiline nose, and the long bony fingers of the right hand are shaped like a claw. Such was the image which impressed itself on European audiences in his later life and which fitted so closely the reputation he had by then acquired of being a man of mystery. It may be that the early realization of his extraordinary talent and the ease with which he could transform a noisy Italian theatre-crowd into a spell-bound, breathless audience convinced Niccolo that the occultist was another rôle which would suit his dramatic style. Moreover, it isn't beyond the bounds of possibility that he did possess a hidden potential which enlarged his talent into the realms of the supersensory.

In his book *Men of Mystery* (London, 1977, p. 13) Colin Wilson claims that '. . . the human mind is capable of directing some unknown form of energy, which can act in an apparently purposive manner'. There is ample evidence that in many of his public appearances Paganini gave the impression of being imbued with a special kind of power, to which some observers gave the name 'electricity', and he himself described it in one of his letters in the same way: '. . . the electricity I experience in producing my magical music . . . and which does me infinite harm'. This experience left him absolutely drained of energy, often perspiring heavily, and 'shaking all over'. Similarly, his habit of relaxing on his bed, without food, for the whole day before a concert and his preference for solitude when on tour resemble modern descriptions of trance consciousness.

. . . occultists believe that if the external physical body becomes inactive, the next 'inner body' is awakened. All of the perceptive processes are now transferred to an area of the mind which would normally be unconscious. But to all intents and purposes it is like transferring one's perception into a living dream. One is no longer bound by the body and can travel according to will. Sometimes, fantasy elements from the unconscious also appear, and these will seem to be equally as real as 'normal' reality.

(*The Occult Source Book* by Nevill Drury and Gregory Tillett, London, 1978, p. 92.)

". . . the most extraordinary person I ever beheld". Paganini by Luigi Sabatelli, Milan, 1813 or 14.

39

He spent a great portion of the day reclining on his bed, and left his room only in the evening, to walk for about an hour. He would pass the entire evening without light in his apartment . . . He frequently remained for hours absorbed in deep thought, almost motionless . . . he left his room with regret and only seemed happy in perfect solitude.

(*Biographical Notice of Niccolo Paganini* by F. J. Fétis, London, 2nd Ed. undated. p. 69.)

Whether, during these long periods of inactivity, Paganini was merely resting his mind and body in an effort to preserve his energy, or whether he was able to achieve a transcendental state of awareness during this physical relaxation which helped him in composition and performance, is something we shall never know. Of course, he was not the first great violinist, nor by any means the last, to practise some form of relaxation which enabled the body to rest while the mind was free to roam; the only difference which would make him unique is that his music-making was motivated by paranormal forces, or, as some contemporaries claimed, by the Devil.

"*. . . jet black hair which . . . more than half hides his expressive Jewish face.*" *An impression of Paganini by José Pinder, about 1831.*

De Courcy quotes (*Op. Cit.* I, p. 131) from the recollections of a British infrantry Colonel (not a breed usually given to flights of imaginative fancy) who was stationed in Genoa in 1814 and who met Paganini there. He describes him as 'the most outré, most extravagant, and strangest character I ever beheld, or heard, in the musical line . . . His long figure, long neck, long face, and long forehead, his hollow and deadly pale cheek, large black eyes, hooked nose, and jet black hair, which is long and more than half hides his expressive Jewish face – all these rendered him the most extraordinary person I ever beheld. There is something scriptural in the 'tout ensemble' of the strange physiognomy of this uncouth and unearthly figure. He is very improvident and very poor'.

This description accords much more closely with the popular image of Paganini than the Ingres portrait of 1819 and, if accurate, confirms that Niccolo had already begun to play the part of the mystic when he emerged as a travelling virtuoso from comparative obscurity. If the Colonel considered his appearance 'scriptural', others thought that he was the living image of 'Old Nick' and Fétis, sympathising with the reputation for evil which Paganini experienced in later life, admits that '. . . The extraordinary expression on his face, his livid paleness, his dark and penetrating eye, together with the sardonic smile which occasionally played upon his lips, appeared to the vulgar, and to certain diseased minds, unmistakable evidence of satanic origin'. In a letter to Fétis in 1831, complaining about the unfavourable image of him propogated by the Paris press, Niccolo told him how he had been associated with the devil in Vienna: –

. . . A still more ridiculous report, at Vienna, tested the credulity of some enthusiasts. I had played the variations entitled 'Le Streghe' (the Witches), and they produced some effect. The individual, who was represented to me as of a sallow complexion, melancholy air, and bright eye, affirmed that he saw nothing surprising in my performance, for he had distinctly seen, while I was playing my variations, the devil at my elbow directing my arm and guiding my bow. My resemblance to him was a proof of my origin. He was clothed in red – had horns on his head – and carried his tail between his legs. After so minute a description, you will understand, sir, it was impossible to doubt the fact; hence, many concluded that they had discovered the secret of what they termed my wonderful feats . . .

If he consciously assumed the rôle of a mystic at the outset of his public career, Paganini certainly paid dearly for it at the end, although by that time this satanic image was closely bound up with many other stories concerning his so-called 'murky past' (of which more later). The points in question here are whether he thought during those early years of his public life, that it would be 'good box-office' to act the part of a mystery-man (with all the accompanying effects – clothes, hair, mannerisms, etc.) and whether, either through over-familiarity with that rôle or through a

41

genuine psychic gift, he imposed on his performances (and, possibly, on some of his compositions) truly magical phenomena.

It may be thought that the evidence already provided – his preoccupation with the theatre, his strong imagination and sense of the dramatic, his ability to imitate – together with the fact, which will become apparent later, that he always had at least one eye on the box-office receipts, is strong enough to indicate that the part was acted. If so, one can trace this line of thought through the rest of this book and see whether it adds up at the end. The dark satanic rôle certainly brought in more cash, and suited him better as he grew older, than the contrasting part of the buffoon. At the same time, it was a rôle which began to turn sour even before he had reached the peak of his career and by that time he seemed unable to discard it. One has heard of people in the theatre who play a highly successful part for some length of time and then find themselves incapable of re-casting. Perhaps this was Niccolo's fate?

The other alternative – that he was a genuine psychic, or became one by practice – is more open to question, although in some respects it fits the facts better. Paganini had inherited a deeply religious streak from his mother, who, as we know, believed implicitly in the vision she had had of an angel who promised that her son would become the greatest of all violinists. This visionary inheritance never left him and throughout his life he was often conscious of future events which were in store, some illusory, others – for example, his early death – predictably accurate. He was also conscious of his 'magical powers' which were inexplicable, in rational terms, even to himself: '. . . there emanates from my playing a certain magic,' he wrote, in 1818, 'which I can't describe to you'. In the early years of his public career the official Italian critics were naturally disposed to compare him with their former heroes – Tartini, Nardini, Pugnani – often, especially in Turin, where Pugnani had reigned supreme within living memory, to Niccolo's discredit. But once he got away from the classical frontiers of his homeland, Paganini's critics were so bewildered by the novelty of his playing and its spell-binding effect on the public that they could only attribute supernatural qualities to him; the words, 'magical', 'Mephistophelean', 'spiritual', 'bewitching', 'demonic', litter the reports of his concerts in German newspapers during the years 1828/9. In Berlin, for example, the two critics most highly respected for their scholarship, integrity, and lack of sensationalism – A. B. Marx and H. F. Rellstab – each emphasized his supernatural qualities, the latter even comparing him with a vision of Goethe's 'Mephisto' playing the violin. The reaction of Goethe himself, who heard Paganini at Weimar in 1829, is particularly interesting because of his intellectual interest in the subject of the supernatural: –

This delightful bronze statuette of Paganini was modelled on that by Dantan. Although the violinist's posture while playing seemed to defeat analysis by most artists, the sculptor has captured here the distinctive feature of the right foot thrust forward and the weight of the body pushing out the left hip.

The demonic is that which cannot be explained in a cerebral and a rational manner. It is not peculiar to my nature but I am subject to its spell. Napoleon possessed the quality to the highest degree. Among artists one encounters it more often with musicians than with painters. Paganini is imbued with it to a remarkable degree and it is through this that he produces such a great effect.

(Goethe to Eckermann)

And in reporting to Zelter immediately after hearing Paganini, he wrote: 'I only heard something meteoric and then couldn't account for it'.

So far we have examined contemporary accounts of Paganini's performance and personal appearance during his early years as a free-lance soloist; it is time to look briefly at his compositions of this period to see what evidence they provide about his public image. The first necessity for a travelling virtuoso was a repertoire which showed off his talents in the best possible light. Paganini had two alternatives, either to perform the works of contemporaries with his own embellishments (a common practice of the time) or to write enough compositions of his own to fill his programmes. He chose the latter, only very occasionally yielding to the persuasion of the musicians to play works by other composers. In Vienna, for example, he played concertos by Rode and Kreutzer against his better judgement, as he later told Schottky, and although Schubert was enchanted by the 'Adagio' movement he added to the Rode, the critics were less enthusiastic and much preferred to hear him in his own music. The trouble was in finding sufficient time between engagements to compose enough works to provide some variety.

The chamber works which he had written during the Lucca and Florence years were obviously no use for solo performance on the public platform; he had to write concerted music which gave him ample opportunity to display his technical virtuosity while providing some interest for the accompanying parts. During the first three years of his public career, when Paganini was touring rather aimlessly through N. Italy, it seems either that he hadn't realised the need to compose prolifically or that some of his major works were written much earlier than has been supposed. According to all the authorities, except Fétis, the only large concerted works composed before his Milan debut in 1813 were the *Napoleon Sonata* (1807) and the *Polacca with Variations* (1810). Fétis says that he has 'an indistinct recollection' of his having composed the first concerto in 1811 but there is no record of any performance before March, 1819. This is hardly surprising because the three years in question are very sparsely documented and for long periods Niccolo's exact movements are unknown. But it seems very unlikely that he embarked on a career as an itinerant virtuoso with only a couple of suitable works in his repertoire and the supposition that at least the first concerto was written during these early years is not completely unreasonable although he may well have revised it later.

In attempting to assess the impression Paganini's works made on his audiences, Fétis wrote:—

I will not speak of the simply curious effects by which Paganini dazzled the millions—of his 'pizzicato' and bow feats—of the modifications in tuning the instrument (he was referring here to the 'scordatura'—for example, in the first Concerto where the solo part was written in D and the accompaniment in E flat) and of the thousand combinations, the merit of which consisted in perfect execution. These will only have a transitory existence and will never hold a place in serious music . . . That which most struck me on reading the MSS of Paganini, that which raised him immensely in my estimation, was the conviction that the mechanism of the art was never carried to the same extent—that he was never equalled in surmounting difficulties—and never was such infinite variety displayed in brilliant passages.

The interest of this passage lies in its insistence on technical excellence being allied with musical invention and variety; the man

Jacques-Pierre Rode (1774-1830)

Rudolphe Kreutzer (1766-1831)

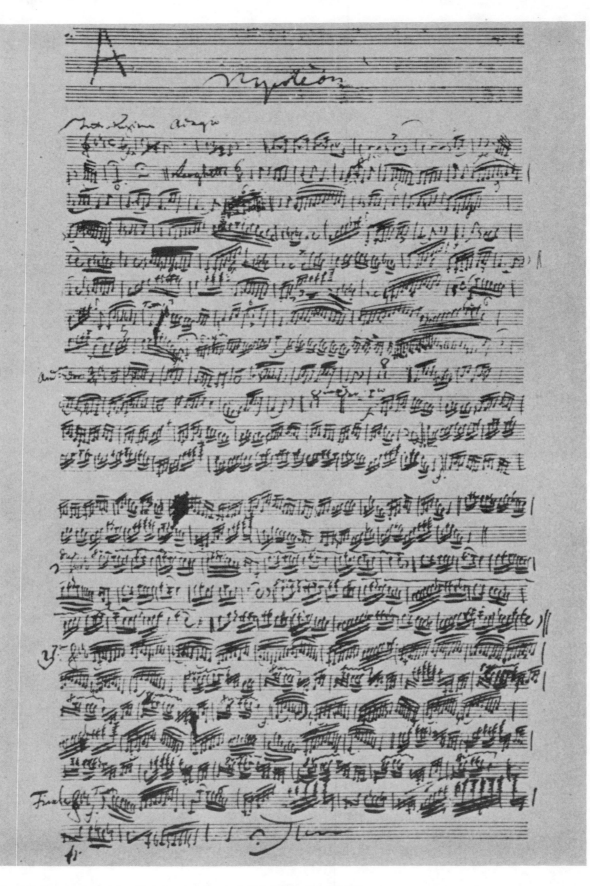

Paganini's sonata for the G string, composed for the birthday of the emperor

was not merely a wizard who performed tricks with a violin but a musician who was a consummate artist, someone who had to be seen *and* heard.

Writing to Germi in 1832, Niccolo said, '. . . no one ever asks if you have heard Paganini, but if you have seen him. To be honest, I regret the general opinion among all classes that I'm in collusion with the devil. The newspapers talk too much about my outward appearance . . .' Was he regretting a theatrical rôle which he had carefully rehearsed in these early years, and perfected in the intervening ones, or was he deploring an occult power which he couldn't control but to which many attributed his unique success as a violinist?

If the spell-binding aspect of his music and of his personality had not played such a prominent part in his career, it would be unnecessary to dwell on it but its importance is so fundamental to what follows from 1813 onwards that one can't dismiss it lightly. His eccentricities were often frivolous but occasionally they had a much more sinister implication. De Courcy (*Op. Cit.*) quotes three letters of the chief magistrate of Dalmatia (Matthaüs Nikolas de Ghetalde) who visited Venice in 1824 and met Paganini there. Clearly a no-nonsense-man, with an astute but pedantic mind, he was at first surprised by Paganini's liveliness and good humour, '. . . when he laughs he slaps his shoulders with his thin hands. He is really very homely . . .' he wrote. A fortnight later he attended one of his concerts . . . 'After the concert we chatted for a long time with Paganini, who was very exhausted. Probably because when he plays, he uses his whole body, and is physically very weak'. Later that evening (how Niccolo must have longed to escape!) they were joined by a doctor who wanted to examine the violinist's left hand to see how flexible it was. When the doctor insisted on attributing this flexibility to his 'mad passion for practice' Paganini flew into a rage. 'It was very unpleasant but we had to laugh . . .' wrote the magistrate, blithely, adding . . . 'How he can have such a demonic effect in the concert hall is beyond me. When he tore round the room swearing, he looked very ridiculous . . .' A few weeks later he heard that Paganini was playing 'every evening in the cemetery on the Lido. So we went over and found a big crowd sitting and standing round listening to Paganini play. Some people were amused but most of them – with tears in their eyes – said it was touching that this great artist played every evening gratis for the dead . . .' On the way home, he describes how a Dominican monk in the gondola told them that Paganini '. . . . had sold his soul to the devil and the Bishop had given orders not to allow him in the cemetery any more because he profaned the holy place'. Whereupon, they threw the monk overboard, whether out of loyalty to Paganini or because they thought the monk was pulling their legs is not explained. Later the same night Niccolo turned up at a reception the magistrate was attending and played the violin again. 'I've never heard him play so beautifully,' Ghetaldi wrote, '... When he plays for us, he goes through no antics. His antics seem to be for the benefit of the public ...'

These brief extracts are enough to show that Paganini's diffuse character puzzled even such an insensitive and patronising observer as Ghetaldi; to anyone who was at all romantic or impressionable, it must have been more frightening than puzzling.

Throughout the three 'wastrel years' 1810-13 (as Miss de Courcy calls them) Niccolo appeared in many small towns, and in some larger ones, in N. Italy – Modena, Parma, Rimini, Ancona, Ferrara, to mention but a few – but it was not until the Spring of the latter year that he arrived in Milan and it was there that at last his bewitching technique and personality hit the headlines. From a chrysalis of obscurity he began to emerge as the international artist who astounded the musical world of the early nineteenth century.

Paganini playing in the cemetery of the Venice Lido, an original impression by John Ruarke.

3 The Virtuoso Emerges

In 1813, Milan was in its final year as the capital of French-occupied Italy. Here, in the huge Gothic Cathedral, Napoleon had crowned himself King of Italy eight years previously with all the pomp and splendour which he knew so well how to arrange. Here, probably in a second-rate hostelry, Niccolo Paganini stayed for six months in 1813. Milan was to become his favourite Italian city and he was to become, in his own way, as adept at the theatrical management of public performance as the French Emperor.

Milan was already an artistic centre of great renown and importance. Of immediate interest to a musician – and particularly to an opera-fan so enthusiastic as Niccolo – was the Teatro alla Scala opera-house in the centre of the busy city. This glorious opera-house, completed only thirty-five years previously to replace the former Ducal Theatre which had been destroyed by fire, had earned a reputation which was far from worthy of it. Artistically, it should have been without a rival in the world: the splendour of the interior, the clarity of the accoustic, the spaciousness of the stage, the permanent orchestra of about sixty players – all these advantages and many others might have drawn to La Scala the outstanding and balletic performers of Europe. But for several reasons it had so far

A modern picture of the Cathedral at Milan.

failed to realise this potential. One reason was that it tried to be more than an opera-house; many of its 155 boxes were privately owned and the owners were allowed to decorate the boxes in their own individual styles, using them during performances as social meeting-places where local gossip could be freely exchanged; in the foyer were gaming tables (the only gambling officially permitted in Milan); the management promoted as much circus entertainment as opera and ballet, presenting acrobats, clowns, tight-rope walkers, etc. for the amusement of their supposedly cultured patrons. Although gaming was finally abolished at the Theatre in 1814 (Niccolo got there only just in time!) a great many regulations had to be made to try to prevent La Scala from becoming a notorious venue for all the dregs and riff-raff of Milanese society. It was failing in its artistic potential.

The interior of Teatro alla Scala, Milan, where Paganini scored his first great triumph as a free-lance virtuoso.

But in 1807 a great effort was made: the interior was refurbished, the stage was further enlarged, and the management found an opera which ran for 39 performances – Mozart's *Cosi fan tutte*. This was the beginning. Five years later – the year before Niccolo's arrival – three new names appeared on La Scala's posters, all destined to play a major part in forging its triumphant successes: Rossini, whose *La Pietra del Paragone* ran for 53 performances; Vigano, the dancer who now turned to choreography; and Sanquirico, the stage-designer whose scenic creations thrilled the Milanese for the next twenty years. The simultaneous impact of these three great artists in the same season must have been extraordinary; La Scala has experienced many fluctuations of fortune since then but it has always preserved its artistic integrity.

Some of Paganini's biographers have questioned why he was so late in coming to Milan, considering that he had already toured most of the other cities in northern Italy. The reason may well be that he knew all about La Scala's difficulties and didn't want to run the gauntlet of its undisciplined patrons until a more civilised atmosphere prevailed. When he did arrive, in the Spring, he had to wait six months before the Theatre gave him a booking. But he must have attended it soon after his arrival because he saw a performance of Vigano's ballet, *Il Noce di Benevento*, with music by Süssmayr, which was having an extended run between mid-April and mid-May and this gave him the idea of composing a set of variations for violin and orchestra on a tune from the ballet which everyone in Milan was whistling or humming. He wrote the work—*Le Streghe* (*The Witches*), so-called because the theme

If Paganini was opportunist enough to cash in on a popular tune in writing his "Le Streghe" Variations, others could do the same to him! This cover-page for a piano arrangement of the tune is dedicated to Antonio Pacini, a friend of Paganini and a publisher in Paris. He published a number of Paganini's early works in 1829. Reproduced by courtesy of the Trustees of the British Museum.

49

heralded the arrival of the witches in the ballet – during the following six months and played it at his first concert. It is generally listed as Opus 8 in Paganini's collected works and was published posthumously in 1851, by Schonenberger in Paris and Schott in Mainz, together with eight other works which included the D major and B minor concertos. *Le Streghe* was the first set of variations which Paganini wrote for violin and orchestra; it established a pattern for future works of this kind – for example, *Nel cor più non mi sento* – in which he took a theme from a popular opera or ballet, or from a national folk-tune which everyone knew – for example, *The Carnival of Venice*, based on the Venetian air 'O Mamma, mamma cara' – and added variations which showed off the violin in his own particular style. Above all, *Le Streghe* is memorable because it launched Paganini on his dazzling career as a virtuoso.

To appreciate the impact which this work made on the public and the effect of this on Paganini's career, we should remember that until he appeared in Milan he was virtually unknown outside Genoa, Lucca, and the other smaller towns in northern Italy, where he had performed his compositions for solo violin or for violin and piano. In these recitals he had 'played to the gallery', imitating not only the sighs and groans of lovers (as in the *Duetto Amoroso*) but also the mewing of cats, the twittering of birds, the howling of dogs, and the weeping of old women. The gallery loved it – usually. But there is one accredited story of an occasion in Ferrara (the date was January 1812 – over a year before he arrived in Milan) when he made a serious error of judgement. He was performing with the help, as usual, of one or two other artists but this time the soprano unaccountably failed to turn up, and her place had to be taken by a ballerina who, although accompanied by Niccolo on the guitar, made such a poor impression that some of the audience hissed. When Niccolo, infuriated by the insult, concluded the recital with his usual zoomorphic pot-pourri, he imitated a donkey braying and told the audience it was a repayment for their hissing, no doubt expecting this ribald little piece of repartee to go down well. But he evidently didn't know that the people of Ferrara were known as 'donkeys' throughout the neighbouring districts, because of their slowness, and the very mention of the word was dynamite in that town. The audience responded furiously, threatening to tear the Maestro and his poor assistants to pieces, so they had to leave the theatre in a hurry and were later ignominiously ordered out of the town by the police. Paganini gave Ferrara a wide berth in the future.

However, the temptation to exploit and vulgarize the exhibitionist side of his technique remained with him and even in his later years, when he was an established artist, he couldn't resist it for long. He was, after all, a man born of the people and their

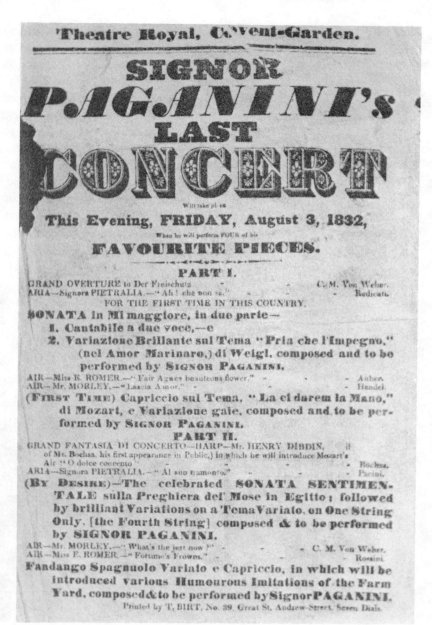

The programme of Niccolo's "last" London concert. Notice that even at this stage in his career he couldn't resist doing his imitations of "the farmyard." The "Fandango Spagnolo" was an early work for which no manuscript is known to exist.

simple pleasure in his deceptively simple tricks of imitation gave him pleasure too. It also gave him a large share (usually about sixty per cent) of the box-office receipts. One can readily appreciate the inducement of tumultuous applause from an excited Italian crowd packed into the suffocating gallery of a small provincial theatre, even to a musician of high integrity, if this was obtainable by the combination of talent on the violin with talent for mimicry. Paganini's audiences in these early years in northern Italy were for the most part uneducated in the purer forms of musical taste,

51

Although R. Hamerton, who
also made this well known
sketch during one of Paganini's
visits to London, was a much
less famous artist than
Landseer, he made a better job
of it than Queen Victoria's
favourite painter. Among the
other musicians on the stage is
Dragonetti, the renowned
double-bass player.

uninhibited in their response to performers, and eager to indulge a
new star; the symptoms are familiar to us in the age of modern 'pop'
music. He may have acquired a façade of good manners, gentle
speech, and proper deportment at the Tuscan court but this was
merely skin-deep and quickly fell away when excitement brought
out the natural personality. The background from which he
emerged as an artist smelt strongly of garlic and echoed to the
shouts of *la plebe*; he shouldn't be criticized for not forgetting it.

But Milan was different. The city was altogether more
sophisticated than those which he had so far experienced. There
were many foreign press correspondents in Milan who sent reports
on musical events in the city back to their own countries. Among
these was Peter Lichtenthal, correspondent of a Leipzig newspaper,

Even serious artists were
tempted to try sketching
Paganini in action because of
his magnetic stage-presence.
This is an effort by Sir Edwin
Landseer, a celebrated English
painter of sentimental animal
subjects. He probably sketched it
when he went, as a young man of
25, to hear the violinist play in
London in 1832.

who, fifteen years later, was to be the recipient of a Paganini autobiographical sketch. His report on Paganini's Milan début is particularly revealing because it distinguishes between his performance of his own music and that of another composer – Rodolphe Kreutzer – a distinction which can't have pleased Paganini and which he did his best to prevent in the future. Kreutzer was a French composer and violinist, whose music for the

violin – including his fine Studies which are still widely used – epitomised the classical French style inherited from the eighteenth century Italians.

Everyone wanted to see and hear this phenomenal wizard and everyone was really staggered. It fairly took one's breath away. In a sense, he is without question the foremost and greatest violinist in the world. His playing is truly inexplicable. He performs certain passage work, leaps, and double stops that have never been heard before from any violinist, whoever he might be. He plays – with a special fingering of his own – the most difficult passages in two, three, and four parts; imitates many wind instruments; plays the chromatic scale right close to the bridge in the highest positions and with a purity of intonation that is sheerly incredible. He performs the most difficult compositions on one string and in the most amazing manner while plucking a base accompaniment on the others, probably as a prank. It is often difficult to believe that one is not hearing several instruments. In short, as Rolla and other celebrities say, he is one of the most artificial violinists the world has ever known. I say artificial because, when it comes down to simple, deeply moving, beautiful playing, one can indeed find any number of violinists as good as he and now and then (and not infrequently at that) even some who certainly surpass him – Rolla for instance. One can easily understand that he creates a furore at his concerts. However, musical connoisseurs are quite right in saying that he does not play the Kreutzer Concerto at all in the spirit of the composer, in fact, that he distorts much of it almost beyond recognition.

The contrast between Kreutzer's E minor concerto, even 'distorted almost beyond recognition', and Paganini's own *Le Streghe* must have been staggering indeed. The Kruetzer, with its formal structure, smooth cantilena, and rather stereotyped passage-work, would be familiar to the expectant audience, some of whom, like Lichtenthal, would be shocked at Paganini's adaptation which no doubt included the insertion of solo cadenzas for the violin at suitable points. *Le Streghe*, on the other hand, provided them with a foretaste of the 'Paganini mixture' which they were unlikely to forget in a hurry. This short work, of about ten minutes duration, contains most of his technical innovations which were to become familiar to music-lovers all over Europe but which were completely new to most people in 1813. It begins with a short maestoso introduction by the orchestra; all eyes would be riveted on the gaunt but still young figure of Paganini while he stood motionless, the violin tucked under his right arm and the bow held loosely in his sensitive fingers, an inscrutable stare on his pale face. After these few majestic bars there is a short pause while Paganini raises the Guarnerius to his shoulder and brings the bow to the strings with a wide sweep of his right arm. Suspense is held for exactly the right number of seconds: – what dazzling feat is he going to begin with? The bow descends slowly, as Paganini leans to his left and sticks out his right foot, indicating to the orchestra leader the first beat of the new section. But what is this? No fireworks, no dramatic

54

leaps or brilliant runs? No – just a simple larghetto tune on the solo instrument, with light pizzicato accompaniment. Whispers creep through the house: 'What's so special about this? Isn't he going to give us any tricks? This isn't the witches' tune, is it?" The melody is repeated and then Paganini reaches a sustained note on the top string while the orchestra modulates the key in a short bridge-passage. He transfixes the audience with a piercing glare as his long bow slowly arrives at its tip and the single note changes to an expectant trill. Now, what's coming? A violent eruption, surely? With a flick of the wrist the bow starts a perky little tune, in dotted rhythm, repeated by the full orchestra; – smiles all round – this is it – the tune everyone has been whistling from that Ballet – what's it called? – something to do with witches, anyway. Yes, it's a good tune; he gives it again, in a different register; we've heard it three times now – unforgettable. But surely, there's going to be more to it than this? Ah! The first variation explodes – a veritable fire-cracker of brilliant double-stops, runs, and up-bow staccato which is so clear that every note might have been bowed separately. Before the audience recovers we are into the second variation – left-hand pizzicato, chromatic runs and arpeggios in harmonics; the tune comes back, just in case we've forgotten it, and we are lulled into variation three – octave passages on the sonorous G string (how *does* he manage it on only *one* string?) – double harmonics – an up-bow staccato covering the whole compass of the violin (how many notes? at least fifty, we'll try and count next time he does it) – more double harmonics, each one clear as a bell. Now, suddenly, we are into the coda, a fantastic medley of all the 'tricks', hurled across the footlights with complete abandon, apparently. The notes are so fast, the ear can't keep up. We try to watch closely, to see how it's done: no use, the bow bounces on the strings many times to the second, entirely controlled by that seemingly dangling wrist; we can't detect any tension, yet the notes are all crisp and evenly spaced, as if fired by some kind of automatic musket – if there could be such a thing! The end comes much too soon – a flurry of harmonics while the orchestra reaches a crescendo and a final cadence; the bow is whipped off the string and held aloft while the left-hand is stranded miles up the finger-board, the thumb bent backwards as if it were a piece of india-rubber.

We exhale, not realising our breath has been held since the coda started. Wild, ecastatic, applause breaks out – huzzah! *bravissimo! – encore! – ben fatto, Signor*! The lean figure crumples into several awkward acknowledgements – one can't call them bows – he turns to the members of the orchestra who are standing and applauding too, he speaks to the leader and we see a thin smile on the corner of his mouth, he turns again to the audience and his eyes are alight now with triumph, he jerks forward, like a puppet,

55

several times, then he totters off the stage with short steps, as if bemused. Everyone talks to his neighbour as the clapping and stamping continue – 'the man's a wizard, he's like a devil with that violin, it's unbelievable, he must be possessed, did you see his eyes?' He comes on again, and again, and again – the house goes wild with enthusiasm . . .

In the early nineteenth century the cult of the artistic virtuoso was a facet of Romanticism entirely appropriate to the age: exhibitionism, escapism, preoccupation with the occult, vulgarity even, were signs of the times after a long war; in Europe we have seen them twice in this century. The technical brilliance of leading international violinists of to-day, which we take for granted, would perhaps have emerged far more gradually but for Paganini, although he was not the sole innovator of such virtuosity. He himself acknowledged, according to Fétis, that 'he owed his talent to the light that dawned for him when he heard Auguste Frédéric Durand play'. Contemporary accounts confirm Durand's technical facility as 'prodigious' and it seems possible that if Durand had been able to exploit and discipline his talent in the way that Niccolo did, it would have been his name rather than Paganini's which would have endured. It was the imitative genius and the creative imagination of the latter which turned Durand's natural talent into a commercial and artistic prize.

The success of his Milan début convinced him that his new style of playing the violin would earn him a fortune and that he could ignore the sneers of critics who said it was cheap and showy, or the regrets of the old-fashioned who compared it unfavourably with the classical style of Rode and Kreutzer. His common sense also told him that if he was the only composer writing the type of music which served that style, he should stick to his own compositions and not be tempted to play the music of others which didn't suit him. He made this point when he wrote to a friend, '. . . it is foreign to my nature to play the works of others, to perform borrowed material . . . I want to maintain my own individuality and no one can blame me for this since it seems to satisfy the public'. Private music-making with friends was another matter; then he could enjoy the quartets of Haydn, Mozart and Beethoven, as he often did, without fear of criticism. But when he was before the public he rightly believed that his own style, which was new, exciting, and imitable by very few, was best.

His perseverance with this course is well illustrated by his encounters with other violinists, famous at that time, who represented the style of playing which Paganini had abandoned. One was Charles Philippe Lafont, idol of the Parisians, who was a year older than Niccolo but who died a year younger, being killed in an accident while walking in the Pyrenees. Lafont was a pupil of

Paganini during a concert in Germany

Charles Phillipe Lafont (1781-1839), French violinist

Kreutzer, who was a pupil of Viotti, who was a pupil of Pugnani, so that the link between the 'classical' Italian and the 'modern' French schools was a direct one. Paganini made a special journey to Milan to hear Lafont in February, 1816, and, according to Schottky, Niccolo told him it was Lafont who suggested they should give a joint concert at La Scala, to which Niccolo agreed with great reluctance because he thought the public would regard it 'as a duel'. He was absolutely right, they did. The notion of a personal contest between two great exponents of technical virtuosity was a particularly stupid phenomenon of the early nineteenth century which continued into the Liszt era of the 1830's (his 'duel' with the Swiss pianist, Thalberg, is a notable example). But it seems that in the Paganini-Lafont encounter neither of the artists wanted the performance to be regarded in this light, in spite of the intense public interest it aroused. The opportunity to hear and observe two such widely contrasted styles was too good to miss and the theatre was crowded to capacity on March 11th when the concert took place. Perhaps Lafont was foolish to allow his great talents to be compared with Paganini's on a public platform in the heart of Italian *Risorgimento* country; the Frenchman never stood a chance, it was 'pure' musical style versus 'exhibitionist' style and in Italy at that time the latter was bound to win, even discounting the patriotic element. In his personal account of the concert (to Schottky) Paganini said that he began the programme with 'one of my own concertos', an interesting remark because it implies that he had written at least one concerto before 1817, the date usually given as the earliest for the composition of the *Concerto No. I* (see Chapter II). Lafont 'followed with a longish work' and then they gave a joint performance of Kreutzer's double concerto and this was the moment when their individual styles could be compared most easily by the critics. Paganini said that he 'held strictly note for note to the written music where the two violins played together' but 'in solo passages I gave free scope to my imagination and played in the Italian manner' (that is to say, in his *own*). In *his* personal account, Lafont confirmed that they played the Kreutzer exactly as they had rehearsed it but he claimed that when they each played one of the slow solo passages in the first movement, his own 'pure' interpretation received more acclaim than Paganini's more florid one. Lichtenthal, who was present in the audience, reported that, predictably, Paganini was much the abler technician, while Lafont possibly had the edge when it came to 'beauty of tone and fine sensitive playing'. Fétis, who was not present but heard Lafont's account of the occasion later, summed it up thus: 'In a concert at the Paris Conservatoire in 1816, the verdict would have been awarded to Lafont, but with an Italian public, eager for novelty and originality, his failure was certain'.

It is pleasant to record that after this joint concert, which could so easily have soured relations between the two, Paganini retained a high respect for Lafont, describing him as 'unquestionably a very distinguished artist', and Lafont continued to admire and proclaim Paganini's talent, remaining his friend for the rest of his life. Unfortunately, the same can't be said about another encounter, this time Italian-Polish, which began promisingly but ended in rancour.

Karl Lipinsky was born at Radzyn in 1790 and achieved a wide reputation in Europe as a violin-prodigy. He came to Italy in 1818 specially to hear Paganini and finally caught up with him at Piacenza in March of that year. The two quickly became friends, finding a mutual admiration for the other's talents, and this time it seems to have been Paganini who invited the Pole to share the platform at one of his concerts. Again, the event was seen as a challenge, and again they performed the Kreutzer double concerto, Lipinsky's interpretation being based on that of the classical Italian style. This first meeting passed off amicably and, according to Fétis, Lapinsky later dedicated one of his compositions to Paganini 'as a tribute of respect'. But eleven years later, when Paganini was in Warsaw, a violent confrontation took place between them,

". . . a strange mixture of consummate genius, childishness, and lack of taste". A lithograph made in Berlin in 1830, shortly before Spohr heard Paganini at Kassel.

58

brought about, it seems, by the press which exploited the political feeling between the young Poles and the more conservative circles in Warsaw. Paganini's concerts were exalted by the latter group, ironically, while his new style was denigrated by the patriotic supporters of Lipinsky. Fétis dismissed this rivalry as a matter of little concern to the two violinists involved but admitted that 'the intimacy of the two artists ceased' from that time onwards. The incident merely shows how damaging it can be when political issues are allowed to impinge upon artistic ones.

Of more musical interest was the meeting between Paganini and Louis Spohr, the German composer and violinist who was another tireless travelling virtuoso of that time. Spohr had been taught in the German tradition (by Franz Eck) but had modelled himself on the French violinist, Pierre Rode, another pupil of Viotti, so, like Lafont, his model was the classical stylist totally opposed to Paganini's novel, exhibitionist type of playing. Spohr, whose autobiography provides an entertaining but at times rather pompous account of his early life, was simply bursting with curiosity to see and hear 'the wonderful man of whom, since I have been in Italy, I have heard some story or other every day'. He questioned everybody he met – to try to discover what it was about Paganini which so fascinated Italian audiences that they gave him the name 'The Inimitable'; but he received conflicting answers: some said that the Genoese wizard produced the most marvellous sound from the violin that had ever been heard, others said it was all a series of clever tricks – he was a charlatan who debased the musical art. These answers naturally increased Spohr's curiosity (and anxiety?) all the more. He was further intrigued (and relieved?) to hear that Paganini's virtuosity could be traced to 'a four-year imprisonment to which he was condemned for strangling his wife in a fit of violent rage'. While he did not give credence to these scandalous stories, one can detect in Spohr's comments a certain smug self-righteousness and a wary eye for his own interests: –

Through his ungracious and rude behaviour he has alienated many of the local music patrons, and whenever I've played something for them at my house, they have extolled me to the skies at the expense of Paganini in order to injure him, which is not only very unjust (since a parallel can never be drawn between two artists of such divergent styles) but is also detrimental to me because it turns all Paganini's friends and admirers into my enemies. His adversaries have published an open letter in the paper in which they say that my playing has recalled the style of their veteran violinists, Pugnani and Tartini, whose great and dignified manner of playing is now a lost art in Italy and has had to make way for the trifling and childish style of their contemporary virtuosos, while the Germans and the French have understood how to adapt to contemporary taste this noble, chaste style of playing. This letter, which was published without my knowledge, will do me harm rather than good with the public, for the

Venetians are now firmly convinced that Paganini has absolutely no peers, much less any superiors.

While Spohr was still in Venice, in October, 1819, Paganini cut short a visit to Trieste in order to hear him play. Early the next morning, Spohr related: –

Paganini came to see me to say many nice things to me about my concert. I begged him very urgently to play something for me, and several musical friends who were present joined their entreaties to mine, but he flatly refused, saying that he had had a fall which he still felt in his arms. Afterwards when we were alone and I pressed him again, he said that his style was calculated for the general masses and never failed in its effect; but if he were to play something for me, he would have to adopt a different style and he was now far too little in practice for this. However, we would very likely meet in Rome or Naples and then he would no longer refuse. I shall therefore probably have to leave without having heard this wizard.

Eleven years later, Paganini came to Kassel, where Spohr was Director of the court orchestra, and gave two concerts. The opportunity for a detailed study of his now famous rival was at last given to Spohr and his account of it confirms that these two giants of the violin-world were totally different in personality as well as in their style of playing: –

I heard Paganini with the greatest interest in the two concerts he gave in Kassel. His left hand, the purity of his intonation, and his G string are admirable. In his compositions and his style of interpretation there is a strange mixture of consummate genius, childishness, and lack of taste, so that one is alternately charmed and repelled. In my own case the total impression, especially after frequent hearings, was by no means satisfying and I've no desire to hear him again. On the second Whitsun holiday he was my guest in Wilhelmshöhe and was in very gay spirits, in fact quite boisterously so. My Faust was given in the evening; he heard it for the first time and it seemed to interest him greatly.*

By this time both Spohr and Paganini were successful enough, in their different ways, not to be jealous of each other; the patronising tone of Spohr's criticism, with its lofty contempt for the Italian's style, was already familiar to Paganini and seems to have made little impression on him. Although he was always extremely sensitive to criticism of his actual playing, he never complained about comparisons between his own particular style and that of the 'classicists', even if they were detrimental to himself, once he had established his name in Europe. He had perfected his own style at an early age to such a degree that from about 1800 it's doubtful if he could have reverted to the classical style, even if he had wanted to.

*From *The Autobiography of Louis Spohr.*

Ludwig (Louis) Spohr (1784-1859), at two stages of his life

Exterior and interior of the Teatro alla Scala in Milan

After the success of his Milan début there was no need for a change of style; he was set on a course of rising popularity and success, provided he played his cards correctly. But when he left Milan in the new year of 1814 Niccolo spent two rather desultory years plotting an uncharted, and relatively undocumented, course between his home base in Genoa and other cities in the north. The reason for this apparent lull in his career at the very moment when one would have expected a triumphant surge forward was undoubtedly the unsettled state of the country and the difficulties of travel. Napoleon's abdication in April threw Italy once more into turmoil; the Bourbon monarchy was restored in Naples and Sicily, the Pope reigned over the central States, Liguria (which now included Genoa) was given to the King of Sardinia, and Austria reclaimed Tuscany and Venetia. Anyone who had had connections with the despised Corsican (as Paganini had in Lucca) was under suspicion and for an itinerant musician of his somewhat elusive past it must have been difficult to obtain the necessary permits to travel from the autocratic and bigoted authorities. In addition, the roads, which were always bad, had been made much worse by the ravages of war. No doubt these restrictions account for Niccolo's temporary failure to capitalize on his triumph in Milan.

But he needn't have made matters worse, and possibly jeopardised his whole career, by committing a strange indiscretion with a girl in his native city at this time. Angelina Cavanna was a young prostitute who succeeded, under the tuition of her impecunious father, in hoaxing Niccolo into a promise of marriage. In view of his long and gregarious experience with this type of woman, it seems that either he must have initially felt more deeply for her than for the others or she must have been exceptionally well versed by her parent and Niccolo must have been in a careless mood when the promise was made. After a while they went off together to Parma and it was there that, discovering she was pregnant, he packed her off to a relation at Fumeri, returning himself to Genoa. Three months later, Cavanna *père* brought an action against him for rape and abduction; he was arrested and imprisoned by the police for over a week until the case came to court. There his lawyer obtained his release on condition he payed Cavanna 1,200 lire. An astounding development then occurred: Niccolo brought a counter-suit against Cavanna (presumably as a belated attempt to salvage his reputation) but resumed friendly relations with the family and, according to Cavanna's later complaint, even made another promise to marry Angelina and to provide for the child; when she had a stillbirth, however, he attempted finally to terminate the association. A long series of suits and counter-suits followed, in which Niccolo was represented by Luigi Germi, whose excellence as an amateur musician may not then have been matched by his professional expertise as a lawyer, since in the end Niccolo had to pay up an exorbitant sum. But if, as may be a fact, his close friendship with Germi dates from this incident, he was not really the loser because the lawyer turned out to be an invaluable friend, acting on Niccolo's behalf in Genoa for many years while the latter was on tour and apparently enduring with patience the extravagant demands made on him. Their correspondence forms the basis of much evidence in de Courcy's biography.

If the breach-of-promise affair with Angelina (is W. S. Gilbert's heroine in *Trial by Jury* a mere nominal coincidence?) says little for Niccolo's discretion and even less for his moral scruples, it seems that he failed to learn an enduring lesson from it. During the following decade he was very susceptible to female charms and equally improvident in his lack of resistance to them. The letters

". . . Paganini remained a child in his relationships with the opposite sex . . . when his own pride and feelings were hurt he cried out in indignation and demanded revenge." This lithograph by Sharp from a drawing by Maurin, dated 1831, depicts some of these characteristics. Reproduced by courtesy of the Trustees of the British Museum.

which he wrote to his friend Germi provided that lawyer with a catalogue no less impressive than the one Leporello compiled on the exploits of his promiscuous master. Paganini remained a child in his relationships with the opposite sex and seems to have been incapable of establishing lasting friendships with women based on deep feeling and mutual understanding. His mercurial temperament and unworldly innocence in his dealings with other people no doubt explains much of the trouble in which he landed himself but it doesn't excuse it because when his own pride and feelings were hurt he cried out in indignation and demanded revenge.

Niccolo's letters at this time speak of his boredom and loneliness. His father — that terror of his youth — died in April, 1817, and it was upon Niccolo's shoulders, rather than on the less musically gifted elder son's, that the burden and responsibility of providing for his mother and sisters fell. At first, he struggled to make a living by promoting his own concerts in the familiar towns and cities within reach of Genoa but he was dependent on the fickle co-operation of theatre-owners who were more concerned with feeding their noisy and ignorant patrons with second-rate opera than with solo recitals. More often than not he had to be content with a short 'intermezzo' engagement, sandwiched between the acts of an opera or ballet. Sometimes he was asked to play in the salon of a music-patron's house and on these occasions he came in contact with Austrian musicians and officials, some of whom suggested that he should give Vienna and other cities in the Empire a chance to appreciate his talent. Although he flinched from throwing himself on the mercies of the Viennese public at this stage, the idea of crossing those mountains to the north — a dream from his early youth — now became a distinct possibility and he began to lay careful plans in preparation. He applied for an Austrian passport, gave concerts in Venice and Trieste — cities which were virtually Austrian in culture and from which he could rely on reports being transmitted to the capital — and even composed a Sonata entitled *Marie Louisa* (to be played on the G string, like the earlier one entitled *Napoleon*). He also purchased, at about this time, a fine Stradivarius violin (his first acquisition of this kind from his own resources) which he doubtless thought would enhance his prestige, if not his performance.* Strangely, when he finally went to Vienna, he left this Strad. in the care of his Genoese banker, taking only his Guarnerius with him.

At Bologna, in the summer of the following year, he met Rossini who introduced him to his impressario, Domenico Barbaja, a self-

---

*This violin, dated 1724, was later sold by Paganini's son, Achilles, and eventually, after passing through many hands, became one of the instruments used by the Paganini Quartet in America (for details see De Courcy, *Op. Cit.* II 388-9).

made man of humble origin who later on helped to promote Niccolo in Vienna. Then in November he arrived in Rome, describing it as a city 'which surpasses the liveliest imagination'. For three months he hung about waiting with increasing frustration for permission from the Papal authorities to give a concert, an experience which tested his lively imagination to the utmost, until at last he was allowed to make one single appearance (February 5th, 1819). His success was so great that two more concerts were allowed before Lent, a remarkable triumph. Rome conquered, he moved down to Naples, reputedly the most difficult city in Italy for an instrumentalist to be accepted because the Neapolitans loved only opera. But when they heard Paganini all their traditions collapsed; they applauded wildly. Not surprisingly, he described the city as 'beautiful, enchanting' and praised the climate, the scenery, the food and wine, the carriages, the public parks, and, of course, the women! By the end of the year he had added Palermo to his list of conquests, been invited to Vienna by Metternich, and was writing happily to Germi about the prospects of marriage.

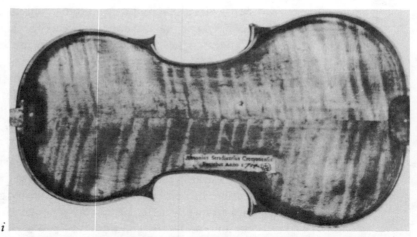

i

Paganini began collecting instruments by Stradivari and other great Italian luthiers when he had money to spare. Some of these he later sold but he appreciated their fine workmanship. i. The inside of the "Delfino" violin, 1714. ii. The inside of the "Kreisler" violin, 1711. iii. The "Hellier" violin, 1679. Reproduced by kind permission of Libreria del Convegno, publishers of "The 'Secrets' of Stradivari" by S. F. Sacconi.

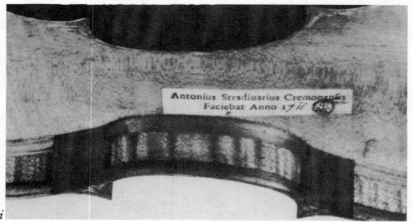

ii

Yet it was while he was in Sicily, where he remained until the Spring of 1820, that he was made aware he was suffering from a serious complaint and thus began that constant preoccupation with his health which never left him. Venereal infection was later diagnosed as the cause of his illness and the prescribed treatment of

iii

65

large doses of opium and mercury, combined with drastic purging and bleeding, began its disastrous course.

After a further successful and prolonged visit to Naples, Niccolo returned to Rome (January, 1821) just in time to rescue Rossini from a fiasco by directing the rehearsal and first two performances of his opera *Mathilde de Shabran*, as the official conductor died suddenly just before the rehearsal and no other substitute could be found. By all accounts, he made a very good job of it and earned the undying gratitude of the composer.*

---

*The humourous Rossini is reported to have said that he had cried only three times in his life: the first when one of his operas failed, the second when he dropped a roast turkey into the river on a picnic, and the third when he first heard Paganini play.

Paganini arrived in Rome in 1821 just in time to help at the Opera by conducting the first two performances of "Mathilde de Shabran", an unsuccessful work with music by Rossini, pictured here. The two men, who shared a strong sense of humour, remained firm friends and Rossini was later able to help Paganini in Vienna.

The following two years cover another low trough in the graph of Paganini's career and the reason for his lack of activity must have been his poor health. He may have inherited tuberculosis and he certainly acquired syphilis, though to what extent his persistent cough, poor digestion, and occasional high fevers were attributable to one or the other – or to the remedies he so eagerly followed – is open to argument (the matter is discussed in Chapter VI). In 1822 he began a course of treatment prescribed by Dr. Sira Borda, a distinguished professor of medicine at the University of Pavia, which involved the internal and external application of mercury and the taking of opium. He had an attack of jaundice – possibly from drinking too much ass's milk – while he was in Pavia but was well enough to return home to Genoa with his mother in October. There he remained until the following summer, when he appeared in Milan and had further treatment from Dr. Borda, in whom he was rapidly losing confidence. Happening to meet another doctor, an Austrian named Spitzer, in a café, he poured out his troubles to him and was delighted to be advised to abandon the Borda treatment and to 'eat only good grilled veal chops and good wine', a drastic change of course which at first did him good and which he described as 'a miracle'. Morale restored, he spent several months enjoying himself with friends at Cernobbio on Lake Como before returning to Milan in high spirits to give a very successful recital at La Scala (April 23rd, 1824).

But it was not long after this that he began taking some medicine, known as 'Leroy's Cure', which originated in Paris. This medicine – described, as the advertisement shows, as a purgative designed to attack the *cause* of illness – had already been through a

By 1822 Paganini's health was already seriously damaged. These two portraits of 1822 and 1824, however, show nothing of this. The latter describes him as the "inimitable violinist".

LA
MEDECINE CURATIVE,
OU
LA PURGATION
DIRIGÉE CONTRE LA *CAUSE* DES MALADIES,
RECONNUE ET ANALYSÉE DANS CET OUVRAGE;

PAR LEROY, CHIRURGIEN-CONSULTANT.

ONZIÈME ÉDITION,
Revue, corrigée et augmentée.

OUVRAGE DIVISÉ EN TROIS PARTIES.

PREMIÈRE PARTIE.

Avec sa Curative,
On peut avoir son Médecin *chez soi.*
Par un homme qui a reconnu cette vérité.

Se trouve, à PARIS,
Maison de l'AUTEUR, rue de Seine, nº 49, faubourg
Saint-Germain.

IMPRIMERIE DE NICOLAS-VAUCLUSE.
1823.

PRIX DE CET OUVRAGE : chez l'Auteur. Par la poste.

		f. c.	f. c.
Broché.	1ᵉ. Partie	3	3 80
	2ᵉ. Partie	2 25	3
	3ᵉ. Partie	2 25	3
	Les trois ensemble.	6 50	8 80
Relié.	1ᵉ. Partie avec portrait des auteurs	5	
	Chacune des autres		
	Parties en sus.	1 50	

☞ Tous les exemplaires de cet ouvrage sont revêtus de ma signature, comme ci-dessous, à l'effet, d'après la loi, de pouvoir poursuivre devant les tribunaux, tout auteur de contre-faction et de mutilations.

☞ La cupidité et la fraude s'accordent merveilleusement avec l'envie de nuire aux succès de la *Médecine Curative*. Rien n'est sacré pour des hommes sans délicatesse. Les uns achètent les bouteilles vides qui ont contenu les médicamens du Pharmacien COTTIN, mon gendre, en possession, depuis long-temps, de préparer les évacuans de ma méthode, et les remplissent d'une composition quelconque ; les autres contrefont les étiquettes et la signature de ce Pharmacien, apposée sur chacune d'elles et sur le cachet de ses bouteilles ; et sous son nom et sous le mien, ils jettent dans le public des médicamens non moins suspects les uns que les autres. Un autre se couvre d'un nom imaginaire, mais semblable au mien, et il affiche la soi-disant véritable Médecine curative sous le nom du docteur Le Roy. Cet avis doit suffire pour exciter la défiance de toutes les personnes qui ne veulent point être trompées. C'est à celles qui préféreront le Pharmacien COTTIN à tout autre, à bien s'assurer de la pureté des voies intermédiaires qu'elles pourraient employer pour se procurer ses médicamens, si elles ne peuvent les prendre elles-même à sa pharmacie.

LeRoy

The "cure" which Paganini began to take in 1824.

Leroy's prices and arrangements for distribution of the 'Medicine Curative'. By courtesy of the Wellcome Trustees.

turbulant history in France. Mr. Leroy had obtained the position of 'health officer' in Paris under Napoleon and had conceived the idea of dispensing medicines by post, with accompanying literature describing its usage. But by 1823 the police had received so many complaints from dissatisfied customers all over France about the effects of the purgative that the Minister of the Interior asked the Royal Academy of Medicine for a full report. In due course, the report proved conclusively that 'these remedies of Mr. Leroy, violent and drastic as they are, taken in large doses, present the greatest danger to the public'. Letters were sent out in 1823 to all the Mayors in Paris instructing, urging, ordering them to prevent the sale of the medicine; the remedies of Leroy, they said, 'must be confiscated in all shops which are not chemists' and even the chemists were forbidden to sell them 'without a doctor's or a health officer's signed prescription'. There was absolutely no doubt, the letter said, that the medicine was highly dangerous and its distribution *must* be stopped. Meanwhile, Leroy himself protested that unscrupulous people were selling bogus medicines in his bottles, with his and his son-in-law's forged labels and seals, thus prejudicing his reputation as a 'surgeon-consultant' and the success of the 'Medecine Curative'. He found new ways of distributing the 'cure', principally through unofficial agencies, and in 1825 the

68

police issued another sharply worded letter to the Mayors of Paris, saying that in spite of previous instructions the 'lethal concoctions' (*funestes préparations*) of Mr. Leroy continued to be 'hawked and sold', and that they were strongly advised to 'take the most rigorous action to prevent their further distribution'.

This, then, was the 'marvellous cure' which Paganini began taking at about the time when the Paris authorities became so alarmed about its lethal propensities and which he continued to take, on and off, for about ten years. (Fétis says 'during more than twenty years' but this is an exaggeration). Little wonder that when he appeared in Europe in the early 30's Schottky described him as 'a heap of bones' and said he couldn't possibly be any thinner.

Paganini.

"a heap of bones". Paganini on his arrival in Vienna in 1828. The lithograph is by Franz Barth.

69

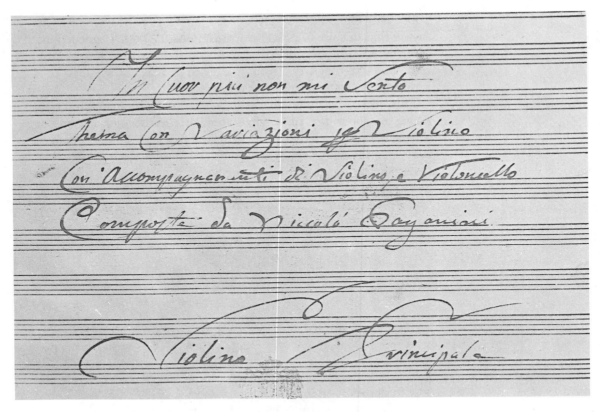

i. The cover of the solo part of "Nel cor piu non mi sento" (literally, "I do not feel any longer in my heart") Paganini's spelling of "cuor" is more accurate than the usual spelling.

There seems to be no evidence that 'Leroy's Cure' was directly responsible for his fatal illness at the end but it may very well have accounted for a good deal of his lethargy and lack of inspiration at this period. Sometimes he didn't touch the violin for months on end and he couldn't even find the energy to compose anything of note – only small works, mainly for guitar (the instrument Paganini always took up when he was too tired or bored to do anything else), between the *Variations on Nel cor più non mi sento*, 1821, and the *Sonata Militaire*, 1825-26.

The first of these more notable works (reproduced here from the manuscript in the British Museum) can hardly be described as a major composition since it consists of a short introduction, followed by the theme (taken from Paisiello's opera *La Bella Molinara*) and eight short variations; the orchestral scoring is very light (violins and cellos only) and the whole piece takes under ten minutes to perform. But after its first performance in Naples, in July, 1821, it became one of Paganini's most popular numbers and he played it frequently in Europe. The second work, the *Sonata Militaire* (so-called because it contains the theme of *'Non più andrai'* from the end of the first Act of Mozart's *Marriage of Figaro*) is modelled on the lines of *Le Streghe*: three short introductory sections, followed by the theme and three variations. After its first performance,

70

ii. The solo part of the theme and eight variations. It was unusual for Paganini to copy out his solo parts with such accuracy.

probably in Rome, this piece also achieved great popularity, perhaps partly because Paganini played the theme and variations entirely on the G string, from which he produced considerable sonority and power besides demonstrating great finger dexterity and a marvellous use of harmonics.

While in Rome, in 1827, Paganini received from the Pope the Order of the Golden Spur, an exclusive and coveted decoration which had previously been conferred on only three other musicians – Gluck, Mozart and Morlacchi. Before he could receive this honour the Papal authorities had to be furnished with evidence from Genoa that Niccolo had an unblemished police record, a qualification which Germi managed to obtain for him in spite of the

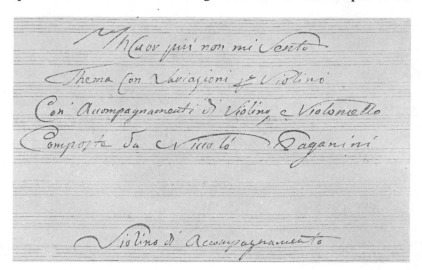

iii. The cover of the violin accompaniment to "Nel cor piu non mi sento".

iv. The score of the violin accompaniment.

Cavanna episode. The irony of the situation was that at the very moment when his Mother Church invested him with one of her oldest and most respected decorations, Paganini was living openly with a woman who was the mother of his child but not his wife; yet at the end of his life on earth, when he had long ago ended this illicit union and had legitimized his child, the same Church refused him burial in consecrated ground for the reason that he was an infidel. Such perverse inconsistency could only have been practised by an authority which was itself corrupt.

We must see how it happened that Signor Paganini, Knight Grand Cross of the Golden Spur, had become the lover of a young professional singer and the father of her son.

v. The cover of the cello accompaniment to "Nel cor piu non mi sento".

While he was still recovering from his illness, he went to stay for several months with a friend, General Domenico Pino, on Lake Como. The General appears to have been an Italian of fickle loyalties; he enlisted in the French army before the revolution, achieved rapid promotion under Napoleon, commanded the French forces which entered Milan in 1796, became Minister of War in 1805, served in Spain and Russia, and was military commander in Milan in 1814; but after Napoleon's fall he evidently joined the Austrian camp and was suspected of being a traitor to the Italian cause. He had married a wealthy widow – the former prima ballerina at La Scala, known as La Pelusina – who owned a palace in Milan and another at Cernobbio on Lake Como, where she and the General retired at the end of the war. No sooner had they settled down there than she sold the estate, known as the Villa d'Este, to Caroline of Brunswick, Princess of Wales, whose hilarious occupation of it provided the gossip-mongers of Europe with stories for five years. The Pinos moved to a smaller house nearby, the Villa Nuova, and it was there that Paganini arrived in the summer of 1823.

Where and how the renegade elderly General met the extrovert middle-aged violinist seems to be a mystery. Paganini told Schottky that Pino was 'a friend who was like a father' to him and it would be reasonable to guess that they met in Milan in 1813 and that Pino, a keen amateur musician, became his pupil. The friendship ripened after the General's retirement to Como – 'that delightful country place', as Niccolo described it; one can imagine how relieved he must have been to escape from the pressures of public performance and the worries about his health to the quiet shores of the lake,

vi. The score of the cello accompaniment.
By permission of the British Library.

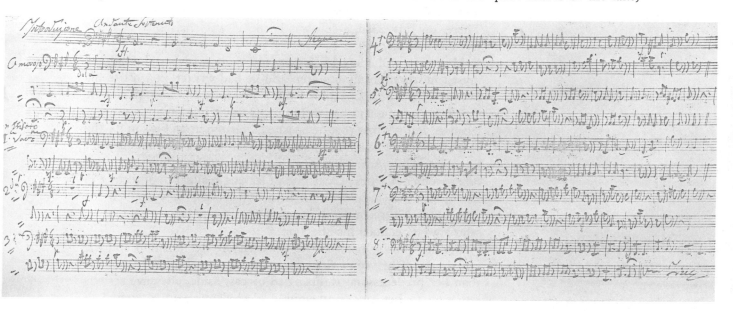

73

where he could relax, write chamber music for violin, guitar and piano, and play it with his friends. But the idyll was spasmodic; for one thing, his health didn't improve as quickly as he hoped and secondly, he quarrelled with his hostess and had to move out to the house of the General's nephew until she took herself off to Milan for the winter. But it was probably while he was boarding with the nephew that he met Antonia Bianchi.

Her home was in Como and, although very young, she had already embarked on a career as a professional singer. Her good looks and vivacious personality made an immediate appeal to Niccolo and when he left Como for Milan, Pavia and Genoa the following year he took her with him as a 'guest virtuosa' a rather presumptuous billing considering he claimed later that when he first met her, 'she was an insignificant little singer' whom he had taught 'so that she could sing at concerts'.

Presumably the new girl-friend was proudly displayed to the family and friends in Genoa before the two of them left for an extended tour of Venetia and the Adriatic towns, crossing over to Naples and arriving in Rome at the beginning of 1825. There they gave several concerts which were poorly attended and badly received; he must already have begun to wonder whether he had harnessed his wagon to the best available mare when at this critical point in his tour Bianchi told him she was pregnant. If he was contemplating a separation from her, as the evidence suggests, this news must have been something of a body-blow; Antonia was a girl of spirit and fierce ambition, she knew the career-value of appearing on the same platform as this 'terrible, weird man' and she had no intention of letting him off the hook. Off they went again – Naples, back to Rome, and then a sea-voyage of three days to Palermo. There, on July 23rd, a son was born; he was christened Achilles Cyrus Alexander.

'My years will glide by happy and contented and I shall see myself mirrored in my children'. So he had written in 1821 to his friend Germi in connection with a previous amourette. Did he aspire to Antonia and her child in this way? The union was never legalized but it's true that he lavished affection upon his son for the rest of his life. The harsh conclusion must be that the *bambino* stole his heart, while Antonia was nothing more to him than any of his other women. Critics accuse him of lacking real depth of feeling in his music; they would be on firmer ground if they applied the criticism to his treatment of the opposite sex, apart from his mother who always retained his affection.

Antonia quickly realised the insecurity of her position and the selfishness of her son's father but she was made of harder metal than her predecessors. Refusing to be cast aside, she gave serious attention to her voice – apparently a good one – and prepared to follow her master as an equal partner in his 'grand tour of Europe' which he promised to begin as soon as he got rid of his 'insupportable cough'.

Meanwhile, the family moved back to Naples in the autumn but he had to wait until the new year before he could give a concert at the San Carlo opera house and he mentioned in a letter before Christmas that he intended to play his 1st concerto, which he hadn't yet performed in Naples. He also mentioned that he had written two more concertos which he wanted to play in Italy before taking them abroad. These three concertos, with the sets of variations he had already composed, formed his main repertoire for the big European tour he was then contemplating—six major works in all. Allowing for the fact that he composed some additional music while he was in Europe, it strikes us now as a somewhat slender collection on which to build a lasting reputation as a virtuoso; Paganini must have been depending a lot on the novelty-value of his music as well as on the hope that European audiences would tolerate repetition if it was to their taste. In fact, the novelty of his first concertos lies in their content rather than in their structure. Each possesses a first movement in sonata-form, developed along the lines of eighteenth century predecessors, a slow middle movement with operatic cantilena melody, and a final rondo. In these respects they are little different, apart from some ingenious scoring, from the classical instrumental concerto already up-dated by Viotti, Rode and Kreutzer. The novelty consisted of the vastly more exciting passage-work for the solo violin; instead of Viotti's elegant but rather dull runs in thirds, sixths, and broken octaves, Paganini substituted bounding staccato runs in octaves and tenths;

A travelling carriage of the early 19th century, reputed to have belonged to Paganini.

75

Rode's exacting but tame trills in the Allegretto of his E minor concerto become double trills in harmonics; three octave arpeggios in Kreutzer's D major concerto are extended in Paganini's to four, or confined to the bottom string. Even the added chromaticism of Spohr is made to sound a little feeble compared with Paganini's breathtaking descents from the top register in chromatic harmonics. But such technical comparisons, which could be multiplied many times, should not detract from the musical value of Paganini's concertos, which is considerable, although the formal development of a theme came less easily to him than the variation-treatment.

After Naples, they toured in Tuscany before eventually returning to Genoa. In Florence the baby broke his leg and the failure of Bianchi to fulfil the role of nurse must have convinced Niccolo that she was far more interested in her professional career than in motherhood. During all the two and a half years they were together in Italy, he complained regularly to Germi about her nagging tongue, bitter jealousy, and uncontrolable temper. Their nomadic and unsettled life must have been a terrible background to the upbringing of a child. Add to that a sickly and irritable father and a highly strung ambitious mother and imagine the consequences for the offspring! There had to be a solution.

Niccolo found it, temporarily, in a brand new travelling carriage for the three of them, a life annuity for Antonia, and the prospect of new territories to conquer with his magic bow on the other side of the Alps. On March 6th, 1828, they set off on the ten day journey to Vienna. The big question mark of Europe's reception must have haunted him on the road but even that was better than listening to Antonia's increasingly bitter complaints at home.

Paganini, about 1843

One of many caricatures of Paganini

The Kohlmarkt, Vienna

A masked ball in the Redoutensaal of the Hofburg Palace

4 The Conquest of Europe

In one important respect the year 1828 was a bad one for starting out on a protracted concert tour of Europe: the profound changes wrought by the French Revolution and the Napoleonic wars had not been properly digested. In France itself, the restored Bourbon monarchy was soon to be toppled by the Parisians in a few days of street rioting; in Belgium, the alien yoke of the Protestant Dutch was overthrown by the militant protests of the native Catholics; in Poland, the patriotic aristocracy tried vainly to throw out their oppressive Russian overlords. It was lucky, for him, that Niccolo was politically disinterested; while travelling in these countries he seems to have ignored their upheavals completely but he must have felt their effects indirectly, even if he was unaware of their causes.

In other respects, however, his arrival in Vienna on March 16th was very propitious. In the first place, his renown had preceded him, as planned, so every musically minded person in the city was agog to hear him; others were curious for less musical reasons since it was not only his fame as a violinist but also as a notorious malefactor which had been proclaimed in advance by the newspapers and gossip-mongers. He couldn't escape, if he wanted to, from the old fables about his diabolical past. It seemed that the lurid and poetic *Tales* of E. T. A. Hoffman (not long dead) were to be epitomised by the human presence of this Italian wizard. The fact that he was an Italian was another point in his favour because, since the visit of Rossini six years previously, everything Italian had been the rage in Vienna and although Barbaja, the opera-director, was about to depart, his promotion of Italian theatre-music had not yet satisfied the Viennese appetite which was still hungry for fabulous virtuoso feats from visiting artists. Niccolo, who had had Vienna in his sights for many years, was just the man to give them what they wanted.

His first concert, on March 29th, was given in the large Redoutensaal of the Hofburg Palace. This great room had resounded to the music of Ludwig van Beethoven in his heyday and surely his memory must have been keenly felt by those who attended Paganini's debut because the first anniversary of the great composer's death had occurred only three days before. Incidentally, Niccolo frequently acknowledged Beethoven's greatness and when he heard the *Seventh Symphony* for the first time, later in this visit, he is said to have been profoundly moved; he often played Beethoven's string quartets but there is no record that he ever performed the *Violin Concerto* – a remarkable omission in our experience to-day but not in the light of nineteenth century neglect of that work. Nevertheless, Beethoven's memory was evoked at this opening Paganini concert in Vienna by the first item on the programme – the Overture to *Fidelio* – and many of his later concerts began with a Beethoven work. Had he been alive at this time it is very probable that Niccolo would have asked Beethoven for a theme on which he could have composed his own variations – the idea had been in his mind for some time and would have been in line with his practice of 'cashing in on a certainty'. But he would certainly have been snubbed for it since Beethoven's opinion of music which he thought was merely showy and superficial was scathingly contemptuous.*

The great day of the first concert at last arrived and although, surprisingly, the hall was not full (the high price of tickets may have

An artist's impression of Beethoven deriding the modern virtuoso – "... putch, putch, putch!" An original drawing by John Ruarke.

*He is reported to have said to a friend (about a piano virtuoso): 'When the real virtuosi played they gave us something interconnected, a whole. When it was written out it could at once be accepted as a well-composed work ... Not like the pianists of to-day who only run up and down the keyboard with passages they have learned by heart – putch, putch, putch!'

been responsible) all the important connoisseurs of artistic taste in the city were present. Did Niccolo suffer from nerves on such an occasion? We are told that he rested in a darkened room for most of the day before a concert, rose and dressed hurriedly as the hour approached, sorted out the orchestral parts (which he had carefully collected after the last rehearsal), tuned his violin and returned it to its case, then set off for the hall in his carriage. This routine was an invariable rule but there were some occasions later in his tour when he arrived at a concert-venue only an hour or two before he was due on the platform. It's hardly surprising, either way, that his platform appearance was scruffy and ungainly: –

Paganini timed his entrances very carefully. This sketch by an unknown artist captures the great moment perfectly.

His clothes flop loosely about his limbs and when he bows he moves his body in such a singular way that every instant you expect the upper part to separate from the lower and both collapse in a heap of bones . . . (Schottky)

Of moderate height, he carries himself badly. He is also very thin, pale, and dark complexioned . . . His head is too large for his body, and he has a hooked nose. His hair is black and long, and never dressed. His left shoulder is higher than his right, probably owing to his playing . . . (de Ghetaldi)

An emaciated figure in old-fashioned evening clothes and long black trousers falling to his heels and flapping about his bony limbs as though he were a skeleton . . . (Lobe)

The awkward bows of his mephistophelean figure, which resembles a lanky black puppet, had a slightly comical effect. (Halirsch)

He looks pale and ill, but by no means melancholy. Only when he is not emotionally excited does the slightest trace of melancholy show in his expression. His dark eyes indicate great affability . . . (Finck)

His fervour was in his hands and bow. Occasionally he put back his hair. When he makes his acknowledgements he bows like a camel and grins like a goblin or a mountain goat . . . (Leigh Hunt)

Self-conscious in the highest degree, Niccolo had perfected a platform-entrance which was calculated to heighten the tension of the audience to the limit. After the overture there was a long pause. At the precise moment when expectancy was about to give way to impatience, he entered, pausing at the back or at the side of the platform to survey the hall and judge the volume of applause. If the welcome came up to expectations, he would do a series of jerky little bows from the waist, and smile. If there were empty seats or if the applause was lukewarm, he would stare out across the footlights with a mask-like immobility of features and move very slowly to his place. Those who were inclined to joke about him before he appeared had ample reason to indulge their sense of the ridiculous when he came on, while those who were curious about the unusual figure they had been led to expect were not disappointed by the strangeness of the reality; the well-studied entrance gave full opportunity for all shades of preliminary appraisal to vent its feelings.

On March 29th, he went through the regular routine. The audience succumbed entirely. *The Concerto in B minor*, the *Sonata Militaire*, and the *Variations on Non più mesta* were the three works he played and the critics' comments the next day were ecstatic: –

Never has an artist caused such a terrific sensation within our walls as this god of the violin.

When we say that he performs incredible difficulties with as clear and pure an intonation as another, when we say that in his hands the violin sounds more beautiful and more moving than any human voice, that his ardent soul pours a quickening glow into every heart; when we say that every singer can learn from him, this is still inadequate to give an impression of a single feature of his playing. He must be heard, and heard again, to be believed.

With each new achievement the conviction deepens that he is the greatest instrumentalist the world of music has ever known.

Succeeding concerts in the capital were received no less favourably: –

The great novelty and prodigy of the day is Paganini. He is not only the finest player on the violin but no other performer on any instrument whatsoever can come within a mile of him . . .

The Viennese, ever ready at that time to react sensationally to a sensation, besieged him in the streets, stuck his portrait in the shop windows, played his melodies in the cafés, and gossiped interminably about his murky past (the imprisonment story was the most popular). The result of all this publicity was that his second concert was completely sold out and the receipts were double those

The Viennese went mad about Paganini and his portrait was displayed everywhere. This contemporary snuffbox is a charming example.

80

of the first. The Imperial Court payed him the compliment of attending an intermezzo concert in full regalia at the Burg Theatre and presenting him with a gold snuff box with the Emperor's monograph in diamonds. The city itself conferred a medal on him for giving a charity concert in aid of some alms houses. No wonder he proudly described these weeks of May and June as 'Triumphs', when writing to tell his friend Germi how much money he had deposited in the Bank.

One of the most interesting, and slightly puzzling, facts about this conquest of Vienna is that Niccolo never visited the city again. Franz Schubert, who attended his first concert, can't have realised how true his prediction was when he encouraged his friend von Bauernfeld to come with him to the second concert with the words, 'Believe me, such a fellow won't come a second time'. By the end of the year, Schubert himself was dead but had he lived he wouldn't have heard Paganini again in Vienna and one wonders why not. If there had been adverse criticism from the musical connoisseurs, it

This portrait dates from about the time of Paganini's Vienna début and his signature looks authentic. He is wearing the Papal decoration.

would be easier to understand. (Niccolo was very sensitive, particularly if his own music was dismissed as trivial, but this didn't happen in Vienna or in the other German cities he visited.) Although he departed from his usual custom at one of the fourteen concerts he gave in Vienna by playing concertos by Rode and Kreutzer, all the other thirteen were devoted to his own compositions – so far as his own performance was concerned – and they were interspersed by movements from symphonies and concertos by Haydn, Mozart, and Beethoven – all the most revered Viennese music, in fact. Yet even in this august company his own works – although providing such startling contrast – stood the test and were received by an enlightened public with understanding. Such ready acceptance of a new genre of instrumental music is much to the credit of the early nineteenth century Viennese and shows greater perception of the composer's merits than has sometimes been accorded in other places since.

A possible reason for Niccolo not returning to Vienna may be that in spite of his great artistic success the city held unhappy personal memories for him. This was because of Antonia Bianchi. His hopes that a change of scenery and the excitement of a concert tour abroad might take her mind off herself proved empty; she remained vain, selfish, intensely jealous, entirely lacking in sympathy for the temperamental artist who had fathered her child, and not even devoted to the child itself. Her life was centred on herself and on her own career as a singer. Genuine love, if it had ever existed between them, had long ago evaporated; in its place was bitter hatred and disillusion on both sides. Fearful quarrels – sometimes in public – and the realisation that the emotional strain was making him ill (he suffered dreadfully at this time from rotten teeth and infection of the jaw-bone) convinced him that Antonia and he must part. Getting rid of her wasn't easy – she was a hard bargainer – but he must have worked quickly because they had parted by mid-April and he had obtained legal custody of the child by the time he left Vienna in mid-August. Antonia was paid three and a half thousand florins (roughly equivalent to the receipts of one of his Vienna concerts*) and returned to Italy where she married a Signor Brunati two years later. They never met again.

We must now pass fairly quickly over Niccolo's tour of Germany and Eastern Europe which occupied him from August 13th 1828, when he left Vienna, to February, 1831, when he arrived in Paris. During these two and a half years he visited some forty cities and

---

*It is only fair to add that in June, weeks after they had parted, he gave a concert for her benefit. It was at this concert that he gave the first performance of his variations on Haydn's tune for 'Got erhalte den Kaiser', the Austrian National Anthem. When he played it later, in London, one of the English critics took him severely to task for making this hymn-tune 'a subject for whining and chromatics'.

Wolfgang Amadeus Mozart (1756-1791), Franz Joseph Haydn (1732-1809),
Ludwig van Beethoven (1770-1827)

View of Paris along the Seine as Paganini knew it

Paganini's son, Achilles, whom he dearly loved

towns in Germany, Bohemia, and Poland (his route is shown on the map) and all this time he had to contend with spasmodic illness and the constant care of his little boy. The latter worry may have helped to take his mind off the former but there were times when he was at his wit's end to know how to entertain him. 'The poor child is bored', he wrote to a friend. 'I don't know what to do with him. I'm quite exhausted by playing with him. I've been fencing with him the whole morning (Achilles was only three!). I've walked up and down with him, made chocolate for him, and now I really don't know what to do next!' But for more than a year after leaving Vienna he didn't entrust the little boy to anyone's care but his own; toys were plentiful and the father denied him nothing, so it's not difficult to deduce that Achilles grew up into a spoilt and precocious boy (he spoke fluent German in a very short time). Did Niccolo have visions of turning him into another virtuoso of the violin? He seems to have wavered on this question but since Achilles showed no particular desire to learn and since he was never made to do anything against his will, the matter was allowed to lapse. Perhaps the boy reacted against the fiddle because it came between him and his companion, while the man had no wish to inflict the pains on his son which his own father had inflicted on him. That he loved the boy dearly there can be no doubt. 'If I lost him', he told Schottky, 'I should be lost myself, for I can't bear to be parted from him. And when I wake at night my first thought is

Paganini's route on his tour of Germany, Bohemia, and Poland between August, 1828 and February, 1831.

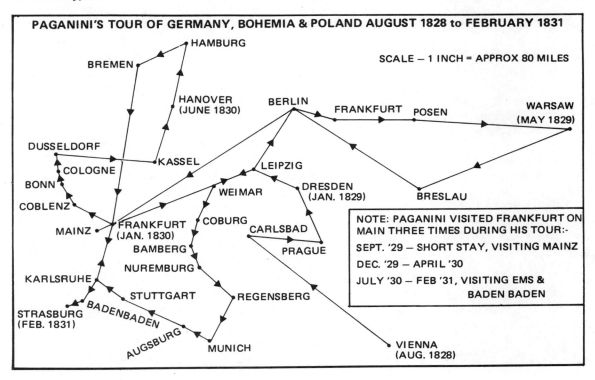

83

of him'. There seems little doubt that he was consoled during the trials and troubles of this exhausting European tour by the thought that all the money he was making would one day provide a handsome legacy for his son. Writing to Germi in January, 1829, he predicted that he would have saved about two million scudi (roughly equivalent to £500,000 in today's money) by the end of the tour. But, he asked, what was he to do with so much money – spend it on fireworks? No, he had a son 'and I pray Heaven to preserve him for me'.

After a summer excursion to the east (Warsaw and Breslau) he returned to Berlin in August. The tour so far had been artistically and financially successful, with the exception of his visit to Prague. In this city there was a strong political reaction against anything which the Viennese supported; the division was caused by racial antagonism. Since Vienna had applauded Paganini, Prague must do the opposite. Niccolo, who was without a business manager at this time, was either unaware of the polarity of opinion or else he misjudged its strength. In the event, he seems to have been surprised and shaken by the adverse criticism which followed each of his Prague concerts; he was accused of bad taste, thin tone, wretched bowing, and even his left-hand technique was dismissed as 'something which anybody could learn with a little practice'. The writer went so far as to describe his performance as 'a harlequinade'. The blow to his artistic pride must have been very hurtful but when J. M. Schottky, his constant companion during the three months he was in the city, showed him the criticisms he shrugged them off with an enigmatic smile. Luckily, his reception in Dresden, Leipzig and Berlin was very different: the critic of the *Berliner Muzikalische Zeitung* wrote that while his technical virtuosity was 'audacious' and 'bewitching', it was, after all, merely a vehicle for his music and what really captivated the listener was 'the inward poetry of his imagination'. True, another critic wrote that 'there was something demonic about him' but qualified this with the romantic notion that 'when you are about to turn away in disgust, he has recaptured your soul with a golden thread and threatens to draw it out of your body'. Such phrases, however ambiguous, must have been nectar after the harsh animosity of Prague.

As mention has already been made of the need for Niccolo to have an efficient secretary-manager on such a demanding tour, this is a good moment to describe briefly some people who served him in that function – shadowy figures who entered and left the scene with extraordinary regularity but who contributed something, whether helpful or detrimental, to his welfare and success.

The first was Lazzaro Rebizzo, an old friend of long standing whose independent means enabled him to travel in Europe with the

This picture of Paganini has been variously described and dated but it clearly shows a man in late middle age and was probably lithographed in southern Germany in 1830.

This portrait, done in Hamburg in 1830, appears to bear the stamp of Paganini's approval. It is certainly more handsome than some others and may have been given by him to admirers during his tour.

violinist as an equal rather than as an employee. They joined up in Dresden and continued together for six months until Rebizzo had to return to Italy for business reasons. Niccolo described him as 'a real treasure' but whether this affectionate praise was attributable to Rebizzo's secretarial ability or to his enthusiastic co-operation in some of Niccolo's amorous adventures, it is hard to say. In a later letter to Germi, deploring Rebizzo's departure, he wrote:

Rebizzo! His name is dear to me and Achilles is always talking of him. He lost the most beautiful moments of his life when he left me. The German belles, who are over head and ears in love with me, would have delighted him also.

Did he remember these effusive compliments when, eight years later, he wrote to Germi, 'Rebizzo, Rebizzo! is the cause of all these woes!'? But a lot had happened in the interval and the tale of 'all these woes' must be left to a later chapter. Meanwhile, at about the same time as Rebizzo's departure, Niccolo signed a contract with a French emigré who had owned and managed a theatre in Frankfurt before being declared bankrupt in 1827.

Paul David Curiol had the sort of experience and personality ideally suited to the job he now undertook. Intelligent, likeable, musical, a good linguist, and knowledgeable about the delicate

85

negotiations required by foreign theatre-managers before a concert was booked, he seemed, in the words of a Mainz journalist, to be 'the predestined guide and friend of this great artist'. If multiplicity of engagements was the measure of success, Curiol certainly succeeded. During the month of October he arranged an average of three concerts a week and the surprising thing is that Niccolo's health stood the strain. The whole management of the tour of south and west Germany in the Autumn of 1829 was left to Curiol but by March, 1830, the partnership was on the rocks. Niccolo must have been an infuriating master because he was continually breaking engagements and suspecting his secretary of dishonesty, apparently without justification. In the end, Curiol sued him for breach of contract and evidently won the case – a common occurrence when people took Paganini to court.*

Next on the list of tour-managers came George Harrys, possibly the most interesting of all and certainly the one who did most to promote the reputation of his employer. Although possessing an English-sounding name, he was born in Hanover, served in the

---

*Miss de Courcy says in her book (p. 334 I) that with less mistrust on Paganini's part and more indulgence on Curiol's, the association might have lasted longer and been more fruitful to both parties than either of them realised. But the situation was surely one of incompatibility and it's hard to see how either could have continued the arrangement longer.

An artist's impression of Paganini and his secretary, Harrys, travelling though the German countryside by coach. Original drawing by John Ruarke.

RITTER NICOLO PAGANINI

The inscription under this portrait ("Ritter" means knight or chevalier) points to the German tour of 1830.

army during the Napoleonic wars and became an Inspector of Military Hospitals until he was forced to retire and devote himself to journalism. When Niccolo arrived in Hanover in June, 1830, Harrys at once saw an opportunity to collect material for a book about him and offered his services as secretary-manager, which Niccolo, having made a few enquiries, readily accepted on a temporary basis. Their association lasted, in fact, for less than a month but during that short time Harrys managed to collect and make a note of more personal information about Paganini than any other of his contemporaries did and one regrets that they were not together for longer. He recorded his master's daily habits, his moods, his manners, and – so far as he was able to provoke any – his opinions. There's no doubt that Harrys must have been provoking; he was equipped with all the minor journalist's notions of snobbery and armed with enough cheek to pierce the heaviest veil of reticence; no snub was too offensive to put him off the scent. It's amusing, for example, to picture, from his description, the two of them travelling together in a jolting coach between two concert engagements (there were at least three a week during this period): the secretary tries to draw out his suffering companion on every subject he can think of – the beauties of the countryside, politics, the people they have met, the latest fashions in clothes. 'Yes, yes, very charming', mutters Niccolo. Or, 'I'm not concerned with politics'. Or, 'Oh, really?' Or just a shrug and a weary hand pressed to the head. But there were other occasions, perhaps in the comparative peace of a rest-day spent in Niccolo's lodgings, when the master was more communicative: –

I've never found it worth my while to deny publicly all the silly nonsense circulated about me. If I please people as an artist, then they can believe all the romantic tales they like.

Some of Paganini's coach-journeys in Europe must have been very hazardous (on one occasion the vehicle overturned and he was thrown out onto the road). This is a humourous mid-19th century print of a coach descending the St. Gothard Pass.

Harrys was unable to illuminate any aspects of Paganini's violin playing because he wasn't a musician but on the personal level his monograph is the most quoted source of information and it's pleasing to note that when they parted in early July Harrys graciously acknowledged that he had been fully repaid not only in cash but also in pleasure.

88

But by the time Harrys was discharged the German tour had only six months to run and Niccolo appears to have spent most of this time in Frankfort and Baden-Baden, enjoying for a short space the fruits of his heavy schedule of work. While staying at the resort (ostensibly to take the waters) he had an affair with a married woman who was the clever daughter of an eminent German lawyer. Ever since she first heard him play in Nuremburg in October, 1829, Helene was consumed by an intense passion for this exciting artist, so different from her boring husband – Baron von Dobeneck. Niccolo was flattered and encouraged her to the extent of spending three days with her (incognito) at an inn near Baden. She obtained a divorce from the Baron and threw herself unreservedly on Niccolo's mercy. 'It's very hard to find a woman capable – like Helene – of such love!' he wrote to Germi, perhaps sincerely. But, like others before, she soon had cause to regret it. He left for Paris, she followed him, he escaped again to England, she remained in Paris but pursued him in her thoughts and letters for ten long years. Hearing of his death in 1840 she had a nervous breakdown and seven years later became a Roman Catholic, entering a nunnery but failing to graduate, and finally living as a religious recluse in Italy to a ripe old age. It's a tragic little story, especially since she was the only woman – apart from his mother – in whom Niccolo inspired a profound and lasting love.

With the new year (1831) came a new challenge: Niccolo and Paris came face to face. In the Spring he took the next logical step and crossed the Channel; not only London but such 'remote' places as Cheltenham, Norwich, Liverpool, Dublin, Belfast, Glasgow, Dundee, Perth, and Edinburgh were destined to receive him before the year ended. Perhaps these English, Irish, and Scottish towns were no more grey and forbidding than the places he had already toured in Germany; perhaps Bamburg, Coburg and Nuremburg were no less provincial in outlook than Bath, Brighton and Bristol. But what evidence there is indicates that the going must have been softer and gentler in most areas of Germany than in the rugged outposts of early nineteenth century Britain. Can one imagine, for example, the peasantry of the surrounding countryside converging on Carlow, Clonmel, Kilkenny, or Cork, as they had at Tegernsee in the Bavarian Highlands, to try and catch the faintest strains from the Maestro's fiddle? And to be in Ayr or Aberdeen to-day on a cold and wet October or November evening is an experience not to be relished by a visitor with no acquaintance in the place; for a sensitive Italian artist in poor health a hundred and fifty years ago, it must have been absolutely dreadful. The marvel is that he survived. It may serve to support the argument sometimes heard that spartan conditions are more helpful to a weak constitution than luxurious cosseting. Certainly, Paganini himself never bothered

The lithographs on this and the facing page were both made in Paris in 1830. They show two very different people. That on the left, by Hahn, is probably a better likeness of Paganini at this time (especially the shape of the mouth after the extraction of his bottom teeth) than the other.

about anything more than very basic comforts during his travels and he was happier when established in a set of simply furnished rooms than when he had to stay in a luxurious hotel.

The first days in Paris, therefore, must have been a mixture of fascination and irritation to Niccolo and his little boy. On the advice of Meyerbeer*, they stayed at the Hôtel des Princes in the Rue de Richelieu, a rather grand establishment, and although Achilles may have revelled in the comfort and reassurance of a warm bed and well-cooked food, beside the excitement of new sights and sounds, his father was soon plunged into the familiar cut and thrust of negotiating a contract for the series of concerts he proposed to give.

As in Vienna, Niccolo was a celebrity in Paris before he had played a note of music in public. Apart from Meyerbeer, he had other friends in the capital who had already prepared the ground and who now loudly sang his praises in official quarters: Rossini,

---

*Jacob (Giacomo) Meyerbeer (1791-1864) was a German composer of opera who had known Paganini in Milan during his 'Italian period'. Now settled in Paris, Meyerbeer had found his ideal librettist, Eugène Scribe, and their first combined work *Robert le Diable*, was produced later in 1831.

90

whose *Comte Ory* and *Guillaume Tell* had been produced at the Opera within the last three years; Ferdinand Paër, his old teacher in Parma, who was now *mâitre de Chappelle* at the Palais Royale; his publisher, Pacini, who had a strong vested interest in his success; and many other friends – French as well as Italian – who had heard him play or who knew of his talents. Nor surprisingly, Niccolo thought there would be no problem in arranging a series of concerts at the Opéra which was then housed in a building in the Rue Le Peletier, known as the 'Académie Royale' after its original foundation in 1669. However, there were complications. The Opéra was about to undergo a change in administration and no contracts could be signed until the new management was installed. Luckily, Rossini was well acquainted with the situation – and with the personalities behind it – so he introduced Niccolo to the new manager – Louis Veron – who engaged him for ten concerts, to take place on succeeding Wednesdays and Sundays, starting on Wednesday, March 9th.

The delirious excitement of the Vienna, Berlin, and Warsaw débuts was repeated here in Paris. A list of just a few of the names in the sparkling first-night audience reads like a dictionary of nineteenth century giants in literature, music and painting: Auber, Baillot, Bériot, Castil-Blaze, Delacroix, Donizetti, Gautier, Halévy, Heine, Janin, Liszt, de Musset, Rossini, Sand. Add the courtiers and the diplomats, the critics and reporters, and squeeze the general

This lithograph, although dated 1831, is clearly based on the Ingres portrait of 1819. No doubt Paganini had no objection to its being hawked around Paris at the later date!

91

public into the remaining seats (for which they had paid double the usual price), and one can imagine the scene which greeted the violinist when, to 'thunderous applause', he appeared on the platform 'swaying back and forth like a drunken man'. After his usual antics 'he stood still again and crossed himself', then began to play. The reviews next day were again ecstatic:–

Sell all you possess; (wrote Castil-Blaze) pawn everything, but go and hear him! Woe betide those who let the opportunity go by! Let the women bring their new-born babies so that in sixty years' time they can boast of having heard him. . . .

First impressions of Paganini, favourable or not, were usually exaggerated and it was to be expected that more sober Parisian

Not only Paganini's fame but also his facial features were well known in London before he arrived there in 1831. The portrait by Maurin, probably done in Paris, was widely copied and this example, in the possession of Messrs. J. & A. Beare Ltd. by whose kind permission it is reproduced here, was probably displayed in the print shops of the capital around the time of his début.

Original oil-paintings of Paganini are unusual, in spite of his willingness to sit. This one, undated and anonymous, was almost certainly done in London between 1831 and 1834. It emphasizes several features remarked upon by English commentators – his large head, long hair, aquiline nose – and one can well imagine those eyes "riveting the attention" of an audience. Reproduced by kind permission of Messrs. J. & A. Beare Ltd.

appraisals would follow. But if the level of critical acclaim dropped slightly, as familiarity bred a measure of discretion, the box-office receipts did not. The first eight concerts brought in over one hundred and thirty thousand francs. Again, Germi was treated to one of his friend's elated accounts: 'It's impossible to give you an idea of my unheard-of triumphs in Paris . . .' And they were triumphs, without any doubt, because although the name and fame of Paganini were already well established in Paris, his style of playing, as we have seen, was entirely opposed to that of the Parisian 'school' of violinists: he had to conquer not only musical taste but deep-rooted prejudices about style and technique. It is fundamental to an understanding of Paganini's career that he was brilliantly successful in overcoming artistic bias but hopelessly lost in trying to counter unjust attacks on his personality and character.

For various reasons, the old story of Niccolo's early imprisonment on a charge of murdering his mistress or his rival had been revived by the press and lithographs simulating the event, with variations of detail, were soon displayed in many shop windows. Instead of ignoring it or nailing the defamation by legal action, Niccolo asked Fétis to write a denial of the story in the 'Revue Musicale'. This justification was so unconvincing, both in fact and in style, that public opinion turned hostile and Niccolo's artistic triumphs were soured yet again. Luckily, before this happened, the manager of the King's Theatre in London, Pierre Laporte, came over and engaged the star for a series of concerts during the summer season. His London début was thus assured and he could look forward to another new experience – judgement by the cool-blooded *Inglesi*.

But it was the hot-tempered English with whom he had to contend first. No sooner was it announced that the prices for his first London concert would be doubled – a common practice in business agreements between him and his promoters – than a furious campaign of invective began in the London press. In vain Niccolo tried to rally opinion behind him through the agency of powerful friends to whom he had brought letters of introduction; the opposition would not be pacified and eventually he and Laporte had to give way, the seat-prices reverted to normal. This unfortunate storm in a teacup, so soon after his arrival in England, did nothing to improve his nerves (already frayed by the overpowering noise of the capital – he was staying at a hotel in Leicester Square) and he was obliged to postpone the date of his first appearance from May 21st to June 3rd. But once more the magic of his performance worked and the newspapers' previous hostility turned to exaggerated praise. *The Times* made amends by saying that:

Nothing can be more difficult than to describe Paganini's performance on the violin, so as to make the effect of it intelligible to those who have never heard him. Hence, and it is but justice to say so much of this extraordinary man, all the anticipations formed of him, however highly coloured, have fallen short of the reality. He is not only the finest player perhaps that has ever existed on that instrument, but he forms a class by himself, and produces effects which he has been the first to discover, and in which few, if any, imitators will be able to follow him.

The Examiner reproduced a long paragraph from *The Times* (which included the above extract) but added comments of its own on Paganini's appearance and manner – 'which, though partaking of the grotesque, denotes a man of no ordinary stamp, and rivets the attention' – together with an extract from Dr. Bennati's diagnosis of his physique.*

The Courier, after extensively quoting Leigh Hunt in *The Tatler*, called upon the services of a Mr. Gardner of Leicester – 'one of the first musical amateurs of the age' – who was evidently so carried away by the unexpected sounds produced by the artist that he

---

*Dr. F. Bennati was medical adviser to the Italian Opera in Paris and a musician himself. After Paganini had consulted him shortly after his arrival in Paris, the Doctor published a paper which attempted to describe, in physiological terms, the reasons for the violinist's unique powers on his instrument. (For details, see De Courcy, *Op. Cit.* II 35-41).

Paganini's London debut was at the King's Theatre in Haymarket, later re-named Her Majesty's but also known as the Italian Opera House. The print of the exterior (above) is dated about 1810; that of the interior is dated 1843 and shows a concert in progress.

described his violin as 'a wild animal which he is endeavouring to quiet in his bosom, and which he occasionally, fiend-like, lashes with his bow'. After further flights of romantic imagery, Mr. Gardner describes the end of the concert thus: –

Though he (Paganini) retired amidst a confusion of huzzas and bravos . . . yet he was called for to receive the homage of the audience; and was so apparently affected, that he would have dropped had he not been supported by Laporte and Costa.

Perhaps the best tribute to Paganini's London début came from the members of the orchestra, who grouped themselves on the stage to

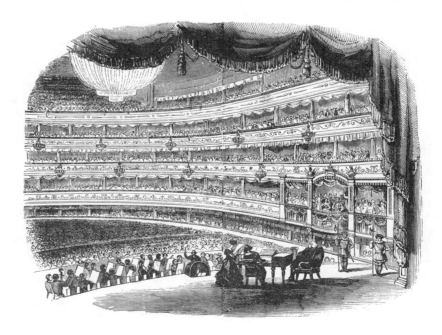

watch his solo performance and showed by their expressions of intense interest that, for them at least, his violin-playing was neither a prestidigitation nor a fiddle. According to Leigh-Hunt, 'they couldn't sleep at night for thinking of him' and one of them (Nicholas Mori) held up his violin at the end of the performance and offered it to anyone for eighteen pence.

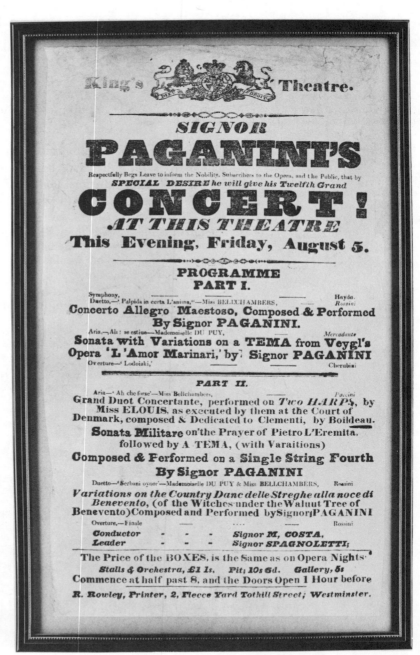

A poster advertising Paganini's London concert on August 5th, 1831. The somewhat vague and ambiguous description of his items was a common fault in England and occasionally causes difficulty now in identifying exactly which of his works is referred to; the first item here, for example, could have been either the 1st or the 2nd Concerto, each begins with a movement marked "Allegro Maestoso".

96

The furore caused by this first concert was not an isolated event; London society needed a change from the political excitements of the Reform Bill, now in its final stages, and even the new King (whose musical taste was said to be confined to an Irish jig) invited him to take part in a concert before the court and reward him later with a diamond ring. Nor were his appearances restricted to places frequented only by the rich; he gave three concerts at the London Tavern in Bishopsgate where seats in the large room, holding about eight hundred, cost only half a guinea.

Elated by his success, as usual, Niccolo left London in July for brief forays to Cheltenham and Norwich, returning in August to the capital, where people were beginning to congregate for William IV's coronation on September 8th. His last four concerts there brought his total earnings in London to over ten thousand pounds. But it was now time to look elsewhere for gold and when the opportunity presented itself in the form of an invitation to appear as one of the soloists at a Music Festival in Dublin he snapped it up. He had acquired a new manager, named Freeman, who went ahead of him and arranged a tour of Ireland, Scotland, and the north of England to follow the Dublin concerts.

The Festival in Dublin was the first of its kind in the Irish capital and was run on the lines of those which had achieved such popularity in England: oratorios, with full-scale chorus and orchestra, conducted by that doyen of Musical Festivals, Sir George Smart*, interspersed with vocal and instrumental items performed

A print of Dublin in about 1830. The music festival there in 1831, in which Paganini performed, was the first of its kind in the Irish capital.

---

*George Smart was the chief member of a family of London musicians who dominated the performance of sacred music in England during the nineteenth century. He was knighted by the Lord Lieutenant of Ireland in 1811. His autobiographical sketch, *Leaves from the Journal of Sir George Smart*, has a pleasantly Victorian air about it.

by visiting soloists. One might imagine that Niccolo would have disliked being in the position of an appendage to such events, rather than their main attraction, but he seems to have been in one of his most genial moods during his visit and, as the *Dublin Morning Post* reported, 'his performances produced as usual the most enthusiastic admiration'. Even his manners, so severely criticized in some other British cities, seem to have appealed to the Irish: 'Together with his unrivalled knowledge of music, he possesses an originality of manner which attracts no small share of observation and interest' continued the *Morning Post*. And when he went with Smart to dine at the Viceregal Lodge he charmed the company with his affability and gentleness as well as with his violin.

After a short tour of the south he returned for a farewell concert in Dublin on October 6th and then, after appearing in Belfast, crossed to Glasgow; he had performed over twenty concerts in Ireland in the space of six weeks. In Cork, for example, the reception had been so enthusiastic that he was persuaded to perform four times at the Theatre Royal within a week. The reviews (from the *Cork Constitution*) make it clear that by staying longer than Freeman had intended, Paganini was influenced more by the flatteries showered upon him than by the shrewd business-sense of his manager.

This print of the Grand Parade, Cork is dated 1840. Paganini gave four concerts at the Theatre Royal, Cork, within one week in 1831.

. . . the astonishing Paganini (wrote the Correspondent) gave a CONCERT at the Theatre Royal on Saturday night, and though we were prepared, from what we read of him in the London papers, and the critiques we gave from them, to witness the performance of a man of extraordinary power and genius of the first order, yet we never could divest ourselves of the notion that there was a vein of extravagance in the description that could not be borne out by the perfection of human

ingenuity in the art. But our notions were erroneously – very erroneously founded. Paganini has not only sustained to the fullest extent all that has been said and written of him, but he has exceeded it; and that to an extent which defies the descriptive powers of man.

To prove his last point, the writer completed his review of this first concert with more general encomium but without any reference to what music Paganini played or how he played it.

The account of the second concert was much briefer but no less fulsome:

This astonishing man gave his second Concert on Tuesday evening, and such was the anxiety to witness his performance, that upwards of One Hundred and Fifty Ladies and Gentlemen were obliged to accommodate themselves in the Orchestra and on the Stage, there not being room in the boxes, so crowded was every part of the house. Signor Paganini was himself throughout the night – his mastery over the violin has left no competitor in the Art. All was surprise and delight accompanied by rapturous plaudits. We understand that Signor Paganini will leave on Sunday for Limerick, his engagements not permitting him to remain longer in this City.

For the third concert, the *Constitution* had a few superlatives in reserve but the supply was running out and the unexpected news of a fourth concert must have been daunting for the Correspondent: –

Signor Paganini's Third Concert
Paganini – the incomparable – the matchless Paganini gave another Concert on Thursday evening, at the Theatre Royal, which was not so well attended as those that preceded it, in consequence of a generally received opinion that he had left town. The paucity of numbers, however, only appeared to give an additional stimulus to the Signor's efforts to astonish and delight; for if possible he was more successful in this respect than at any of his previous Concerts. To convey a proper idea of the display of his unrivalled powers of execution in the Irish Air of Patrick's Day, with variations of his own composition on one string, would be a difficult task for the most accomplished and experienced proficient in the science of Music. The raptures of the audience, the loud and vehement calls of encore, and the enthusiastic cheering that followed, when Signor Paganini responded to the call, were tests of the delight which his performance imparted! . . . This evening Signor Paganini's fourth and last Concert in Cork will take place, and already the Box Sheet indicates a crowded and fashionable audience.

The *St. Patrick's Day Variations* on the Irish National Anthem were, of course, written specially for this tour and as his visit to Cork happened to coincide with the arrival of Sir Edward Codrington's fleet at the nearby estuary of Cóbh, an interesting test of loyalty must have arisen for any naval personnel who attended his concerts. Paganini himself, being entirely impervious to any political atmosphere, would in any case have remained oblivious – intent only on pleasing his audiences.

99

A print, dated 1830, of one of Edinburgh's winding old streets. Paganini enjoyed one of his greatest successes in the Scottish capital, giving six concerts in the Assembly Rooms, George Street. He was relieved not to be pursued in these northern cities by malicious gossip about his past.

After leaving Edinburgh, at the beginning of November 1831, Paganini travelled to Ayr where he was billed to give one concert. But, as so often happened, he decided to stay on and make a second appearance which was badly attended because the town was not big enough to provide two full houses at inflated prices. This fine print of Ayr in about 1840 was produced for an edition of Robert Burns' poems.

The Scottish tour of 1831 was no less crowded with engagements, although Freeman seems to have encountered the same difficulties here as elsewhere in the British Isles – namely guarantees from theatrical managements being dishonoured and tickets being advertised at double or treble the usual prices. His problems were magnified by his master's occasional whims, which meant that he either refused to honour a date or decided to give an extra concert at a place where only one had been arranged; in either event the results were disastrous but created only local furore because gossip

100

didn't spread quickly enough in the more remote places to affect business later in the tour. Again it must be remarked how the Maestro's health and his manager's patience stood the strain; an average of three to four concerts a week is a very tight schedule for a tour, even under modern travelling conditions. But the bracing October air of Scotland (they went as far north as Perth) must have had a beneficial effect on Niccolo's temperament; he enjoyed one of his greatest successes in Edinburgh, for example, and when the Lord Provost invited him to give a charity concert, he acquiesced promptly and with none of the niggling conditions which sometimes marred his acts of generosity in other circumstances and gave him a reputation for meanness which was largely unjustified.

Although he was unwilling to admit it, Niccolo thrived on hard work at this period of his life. No sooner was he back in London at the end of the year than he was off again on a tour of the south and west – Brighton, Bath, Bristol, Exeter – followed by an expedition through the north – Liverpool, Manchester, Leeds, Chester, Birmingham, York, Halifax, Hull. The first of these cities, Liverpool, had been waiting for him for six weeks since the original announcement of his arrival was published; there was the usual difficulty of arranging a venue but at last the management of the Theatre Royal and Freeman reached agreement – the price of admission, according to one report, being 'higher than at any other place out of London' – and at last the three promised concerts took place, attended by 'all the beauty and fashion, not only of the town but of the neighbourhood'. The writer of *A Memoir of Signor Paganini and Critical Remarks on his Performances*, published in Liverpool in 1832, tells us that '. . . Williamson Square was nightly crowded with equipages and all who went to hear him returned enraptured'. His performance is then described by 'a Liverpool critic' as follows: –

We will now attempt a more particular description, and suppose that the reader is awaiting his appearance, as we have often done, with eager and tremulous impatience. He enters the orchestra, bending and smiling, (but what a ghastly smile!) – a sallow, haggard, ungraceful spectre, – with his instrument clutched, rather than held, in his lean claw-like fingers, – you would as soon expect melody from a sepulchre. A few seconds elapse, the burst of applause subsides, and a change comes over the musician, so sudden, that you are already tempted to believe him a sorcerer. His figure grows erect, his attitude commanding, his features stern and thoughtful: he is brooding over the mystery, and you expect, with breathless eagerness its disclosure. With a sudden indescribable motion he lets fall from the tip of his bow, one – two – three – short, thrilling touches, – to set off the band, – and is silent. A like number of sharp pizzicatos follow, and another pause. The orchestra now, upon a repetition of his wild gesture, begin a striking movement, pointed as it were by occasional dashes from the maestro; the crescendo commences, arrives at its climax, and at once from the concluding crash of the instruments, starts out Paganini's long,

Mr. Collins, "The English Paganini" – a print published in London in 1831.

glistening tone, the beginning of a strain of delicious melody, chaste, and yet passionate in expression, woven of notes of inconceivable firmness and delicacy, and of a clear far-reaching power, which searches your heart's centre. Soon the burden becomes more wild and restless, the strings moan and quiver, until he sinks, through a passage of gliding semi-tones, into the depths of the scale, with such a lamenting energy of plaintiveness, as you cannot hear without weeping. His instrument is no longer a violin, it is some living thing that wails and shudders in a transport of terror or sorrow; the quality of its tone, in such passages, is the most wonderful thing we have ever heard, and it will dwell in our heart until it ceases to move. This mourning strain is interrupted by the repetition of a rapid, thrilling staccato, little louder than a whisper, but of such a wizard awfulness that it makes you shiver, preceding short phrases of tremendous expressiveness; – and while the ear is all awake to mark what may ensue, the maestro bounds at once into the mazes of his execution. All that can be conceived, most capricious, brilliant, and astonishing, will nevertheless fall short of any adequate idea of these extraordinary displays: – chromatic runs, such as escape from the ear by their meteor rapidity, – arpeggios, every note of which is swift, distinct, and bright, as the sparks from a firework, – passages of flowing melody, accompanied by crisp pizzicatos performed by the left hand; and long divisions of double notes, rapid, smooth, and miraculously perfect in intonation. After exhibiting these

Another of the well known sketches of Paganini drawn at a performance in the King's Theatre, London, in June, 1831, by R. Hamerton. The ill-fitting dress-suit is well depicted by both the artists reproduced on these pages.

"... his figure grows erect, his attitude commanding ..." A sketch of Paganini published in London in about 1831. It is untypical because it shows his left foot thrust forward instead of his right which was more usual.

wonders in every mode and articulation, you might suppose his art is exhausted. Far from it. A greater masterstroke is yet to be given. The phrases which he has produced in the natural tone of the instrument he now echoes in twinkling harmonics, producing these sounds with such fine minuteness, that Oberon and Titania might suppose them the music of their own court, – whispers of an almost evanescent acuteness, and shakes, like the trembling of a silver thread. After he has thus disported himself for some time, the spirit of the strain again changes, and grows stern. As he absolutely tears from his instrument a succession of fierce, thrilling, imperative notes, the accompaniment bursts in; and when, as you imagine, the close has arrived, the orchestra remains silent, – Paganini gives a cadence, soars up into a fantastic melody absolutely elfin in its gamesomeness, and ends, when you least expect it, with a sudden dash of hurried twittering staccatos that start from his strings like the bursting of a bundle of squibs, leaving you in a state of mingled delight and surprise which is almost ludicrous. He flings his bow upwards, with a wild gesture, and glances triumphantly around, but the fire seems to remain with him for a moment only after the violin has ceased, and he shrinks once more into the feeble object he at first appeared. You draw a deep breath after he has departed from the orchestra, and ask yourself if what you have seen and heard be not a dream.

The writer of the *Memoir* goes on to quote an interesting comment from a musical journal: –

Many are accustomed to suppose that the one-stringed performance is peculiar to Paganini alone, but it is not such a 'rara avis' as is generally imagined. Master Burke, at his farewell benefit here, previous to his departure for America, announced a performance on the fourth string, as being among the entertainments selected for the occasion, and also intimated that it was the first time it had ever been attempted in England; but from a recent number of *The Harmonicon*, it appears that so far back as 1817, Mr. Collins gave many similar exhibitions at various musical assemblies.

Finally, from Liverpool, we have a description of Paganini's appearance at this time which accords with the conception of a man whose body was wasted with illness but contorted by habit and compulsion to perform the function of a musical brain which was inexhaustible: –

His appearance is strikingly peculiar. There is an air of sadness about him, and he seems as if his soul fed upon its own mysterious melancholy. His physical configuration is equally remarkable – tall and gaunt as he is represented, and his neck seems long and his head large. When he stands erect, one shoulder appears higher than the other, and one arm also longer than its fellow. His frame seems fleshless as his picture; and it is supposed that all these physical predispositions have been auxiliary causes to enable Paganini to exercise those wizard powers of melody with which he is undeniably gifted.

The strain of undertaking such an itinerary in the north of England in the depths of winter, even if he did travel in 'a most beautiful carriage' and enjoy the services of 'a most polite English secretary' (Freeman) and 'a most excellent valet', must have been enough to test the stamina of a colossus and try the patience of a saint. When Niccolo also tells Germi that he is looking forward to relating 'the most astonishing things about the customs of this country', one would like to know what he said when they eventually met, if he hadn't forgotten by that time. One feature of the British way of life which obviously appealed to him, judging by the number of times he mentioned it in his letters home, was the country house. Long coach journeys through the length and breadth of the English countryside must have given him plenty of opportunity to ruminate on the delights of retiring to an estate in Italy similar to one of those late Georgian manors, nestling in its sun-drenched park, which he so much admired as he slowly passed it along the road. He is forever asking Germi to give him some idea of the *Delizia* or *Paradiso*, as he calls it, which he has asked him to purchase in one of the wooded valleys to the north of Genoa and he adds pathetically that he needs to rest for a few years from 'certain troubles' which have made him melancholy. Poor Niccolo! He must have already felt a dread of the breakdown in his health which he knew was overtaking him but he can have had no idea of 'certain troubles' in addition, which were still to come.

One of these troubles concerned his concert-manager and was entirely of his own making. At some point in his English tour –perhaps in Bath or when he returned to London in February,

Paganini travelled many miles by coach through the length and breadth of the British Isles, often in winter conditions. This black and white engraving of a contemporary watercolour by Turner, "Frosty morning", gives some idea of the appaling conditions of most of the roads at that time.

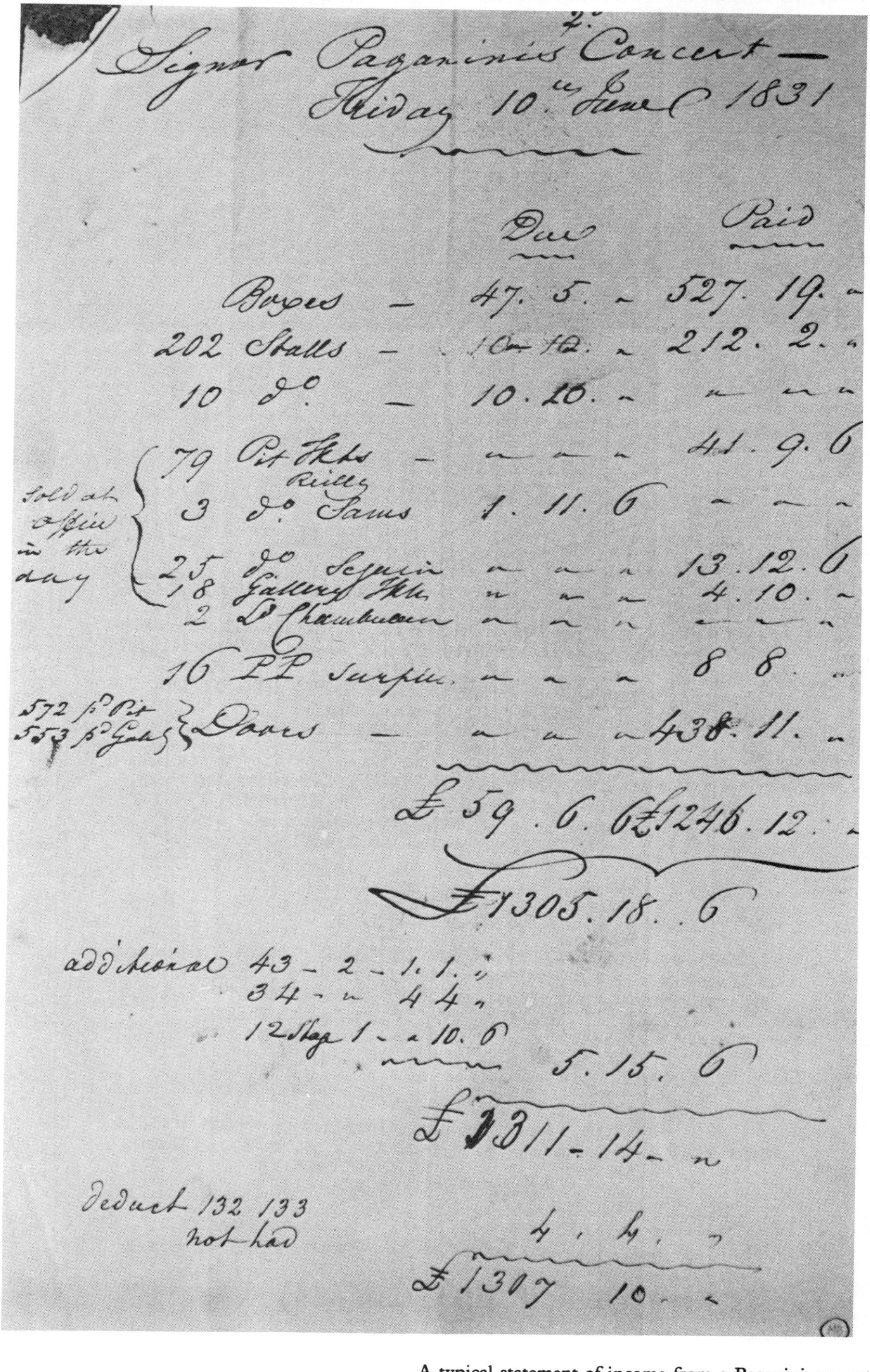

Signor Paganini's Concert —
Friday 10th June 1831

	Due	Paid
Boxes	47. 5. ~	527. 19. ~
202 Stalls	10. 10. ~	212. 2. ~
10 do	10. 10. ~	~ ~ ~
79 Pit Tkts	~ ~ ~	41. 9. 6
3 do Reilly Sams	1. 11. 6	~ ~ ~
25 do Seguin	~ ~ ~	13. 12. 6
18 Gallery Tkts	~ ~ ~	4. 10. ~
2 Do Chamberlain	~ ~ ~	~ ~ ~
16 PP Surplus	~ ~ ~	8. 8. ~
572 pd Pit / 553 pd Gall } Doors	~ ~ ~	438. 11. ~

sold at Office in the day

572 pd Pit
553 pd Gall

£ 59. 6. 6   £1246. 12. ~

£1305. 18. 6

additional   43 — 2 — 1. 1. ~
34 — ~ 4 4. ~
12 Stag 1 — ~ 10. 6
5. 15. 6

£1311. 14. ~

deduct 132 133
not had
4. 4. ~

£1307 10. ~

A typical statement of income from a Paganini concert

SIGNOR
PAGANINI's
FAREWELL
CONCERT

And positively the Last Night this Theatre will be open until the
commencement of the regular Dramatic Season,

THIS EVENING,
Friday, August 17, 1832,

When he will perform FOUR of his

FAVOURITE PIECES:
PART I.

GRAND SINFONIA. —— —— *Beethoven.*
ARIA, Signora PIETRALIA, " Elena, oh ! tu ch'io chiamo." (*La Donna del Lago*)
                                                         (*Rossini.*

**Grand Sonata Militare, in which will be introduced Mozart's
Aria, " Non piu andrai," followed by a Tema, with brilliant
Variations, (to conclude with " GOD SAVE THE KING !")
composed and to be performed on ONE STRING ONLY,**
(the Fourth String,) by

SIGNOR PAGANINI.

ARIA, Mr. BENNETT, " Languir per una bella" *Rossini.*
AIR, Miss GEORGE, " Hours of sorrow." *Rossini.*
LARGHETTO e VARIAZIONE, on the favourite RONDO,
" Non piu mesta," in Rossini's Opera LA CENERENTOLA,
composed and to be performed by

SIGNOR PAGANINI.

PART II.

The CORONATION DUET, for the Harp and Piano-Forte.
   Messrs. FREDERICK CHATTERTON and W. A. KING. *Bochsa.*
DUETTO, Signora PIETRALIA and Mr. BENNETT,
   " Ah ! se di mali miei." —— (*Il Tancredi*)—*Rossini.*
**MAESTOSO SONATA SENTIMENTALE, with Variations
on Haydn's celebrated Tema " The Hymn to the Emperor,"
(to conclude with the National Air—" St. PATRICK's DAY,")
ON ONE STRING ONLY, (the Fourth String)**
composed and to be performed by

SIGNOR PAGANINI.

RECIT. ed ARIA, Miss GEORGE, " Mi pizzica mi stimola."
   (From *Auber's* Opera of *Masaniello*)—arranged by *G. Pons.*
BALLAD, Mr. BENNETT, " Fair is the morn." —— *A. Lee.*
(*BY DESIRE*) **Fandango Spagnuolo Variato, in which will be
introduced various Humourous Imitations of the Farm Yard,**
Composed and to be performed by
Signor PAGANINI.

Leader of the Band, (*with the kind consent of Capt. Polhill*) Mr. T. COOKE.
Conductor, — — — SIR GEORGE SMART.

The Free List will be suspended, the Public Press excepted.

Doors opened at HALF-PAST SEVEN O'CLOCK, the Concert to commence at EIGHT.

Boxes 7s. Pit 3s. 6d. Galleries 2s

Printed by W. REYNOLDS, 9 Exeter-street, Strand.

Poster showing concert of works by various composers

"... there is an air of sadness about him . . ." Paganini, painted by H. E. Dawe, London, 1831.

1832 – he met the Watson family. Charlotte was the youngest daughter, a bewitching girl with a strong mezzo-soprano voice, and her father, John Watson, was the musical director of the King's Theatre in London where Niccolo had scored so many triumphs. Niccolo immediately fell for Charlotte. Her father, whose contract at the Theatre was about to end, persuaded him to drop Freeman and take him instead, as combined manager-accompanist. The change was to prove disastrous. Freeman was no doubt expensive (he was paid a monthly salary) but he had a shrewd business sense and had kept his master's schedule balanced and his reputation as intact as possible; Watson was unable to match either achievement. After returning to Paris in March, in spite of the raging cholera epidemic which had spread from England, Niccolo came back to London at the end of June and gave eleven concerts at Covent Garden between July 6th and August 17th, most of which were poorly attended (the cholera menace no doubt accounted for this). A short tour in southern England – Canterbury, Brighton, Southampton, Winchester, Portsmouth and Chichester – was no more profitable, the receipts falling at one concert below fifty pounds. Back to Paris he went in September accompanied by Charlotte, with her father's consent, and Watson's mistress, Miss Wells, who acted as a rather incongruous chaperone.

That winter of 1832-3 in Paris was an unproductive period, apparently, in Paganini's tour of Europe. He seemed to have reached a point where he needed an injection of new interest to stimulate both his own performance and the public's response. In one of his letters to Germi he confesses to being 'overcome with laziness' and the discomfort which the cold weather brought to father and son is easily imaginable by his complaint of 'faulty fireplaces which smoked' and caused him to change their lodgings at least six times in almost as many weeks. The feeling that he was regarded by the public and by some sections of the press as a transient sensation, to be heard once and then forgotten, that his music was likewise insubstantial and ephemeral, must have brought on the 'ennui' which certainly affected him at this time; he loved the limelight and if the fierce glare of publicity sometimes brought its problems, at least these were more exciting than obscurity. The difficulty was that he had no suitable base from which to operate, no efficient secretary or agent to organize his tours, and no inspiration to compose new music; yet his name was made in Europe and there was nothing to prevent him building up his fortune still further with the aim of retirement in a few years and then bequeathing it to the little boy who was by his side. What he needed now was a revival, an uplift, which would once again appeal to the public imagination and establish him firmly at the very top of the European concert-bills.

105

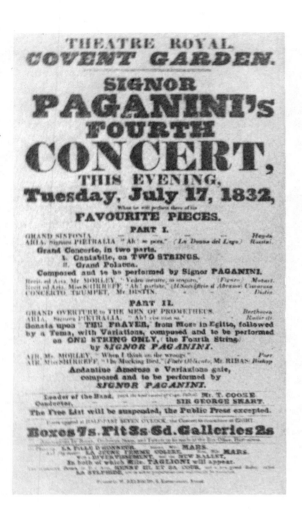

Between July 6th and August 17th, 1832, Paganini gave eleven concerts at Covent Garden. Here are the advertisements for two of them.

At about this time, two ideas occurred to him which were possibly connected with the situation just described. First, he acquired the title of 'Baron', under circumstances which were anything but commendable. The decoration was accorded to him in France out of respect for his being made a Knight of the first class of the Order of St. Stanislas. This high-sounding title was, in fact, nothing short of bogus, since it was bestowed on him, probably in return for a fairly large fee, by an exiled and impoverished German Prince who had no constitutional power to confer it, nor did it carry any hereditary right. The fact that Niccolo was proud enough of this mockery of an honour to announce it in the press and to style himself 'Baron' is evidence of his pathetic wish to escape from the status of an itinerant Italian fiddler and to be accepted by European society as a signor worthy of respect. Although he had made about half a million pounds in the past year, he wouldn't be satisfied until he had earned (or bought) social standing as well.

This well known profile of Paganini, designed by G. Bignami and engraved by Gravigni, was executed before all the troubles of the 1830's had taken their toll.

The other idea was much more creditable and concerned his interest in the viola. This instrument had been much neglected by early nineteenth century composers and since Mozart's *Sinfonia Concertante* (violin, viola and orchestra) no important solo work had been written for it. Hector Berlioz, however, understood the viola's potentialities perfectly, as the following extract from his *A Treatise upon Modern Instrumentation and Orchestration* shows: –

Of all the instruments in the orchestra, the one whose excellent qualities have been longest misunderstood is the viola. It is no less agile than the violin, the sound of its low strings is particularly telling, its upper notes are distinguished by their mournfully passionate accent, and its quality of tone altogether, profoundly melancholy, differs from that of other instruments played with the bow.

Berlioz favoured the large viola, not the small-sized variety often used by orchestral players who were really violinists, and it

107

happened that in 1833 Niccolo himself became interested in this large instrument for which his long fingers and unusually long reach with the left hand were particularly well suited. We know from his letters to Germi that he was contemplating making the viola a feature of his appearances in London the following year (he bought a Strad viola, dated 1731, from George Corsby, and asked Germi to send his own large viola to London*), so it's not surprising that he wanted a distinguished solo work to show the instrument – and himself – off to the best advantage. He was feeling too unwell at this time – the end of the year – to compose one himself (he thought he was going to die in November and a friend wrote an urgent note to Germi asking him to come to Paris before it was too late) so when he had recovered sufficiently to get about he went to see Berlioz who wrote this account of the meeting: –

Some weeks after . . . Paganini came to see me. He told me he had a Stradivarius viola, a splendid instrument, which he wanted to play in

*The Strad later became one of four instruments known as the 'Paganini Quartet', used by members of the string quartet of that name based in New York. For details of this and of other instruments acquired by Paganini, see De Courcy, *Op. Cit.* II pp. 388-390.

The Stradivarius viola, made in 1731, which Paganini bought in London. Reproduced by kind permission of Libreria del Convegno, publishers of "The 'Secrets' of Stradivari" by S. F. Sacconi.

public; but he lacked the right music. Would I write him a piece for it? 'You are the only one I would trust with such a commission', he said. I replied that I was immensely flattered but that to fulfill his expectations and write a work that showed off a virtuoso such as he in a suitably brilliant light, one should be able to play the viola, which I could not. 'No, no, I insist,' he said, 'you will manage. I cannot possibly do it – I am too ill to compose'.

Berlioz had the novel idea of writing a symphony based, loosely, on the wanderings of a melancholy dreamer – himself – in the mountains; being an admirer of English literature of the romantic style – not only of Shakespeare – he called it *Harold in Italy*, after Byron's *Childe Harold*, the solo viola representing Harold. It was a typically imaginative Berliozian invention – but it was *not* music à la Paganini: –

No sooner was the first movement written (Berloiz continued) than Paganini wanted to see it. At the sight of so many rests in the viola part in the 'allegro' he exclaimed: 'That's no good. There's not enough for me to do here. I should be playing all the time'. I reminded him what I had said at the start; he wanted a viola concerto which only he could write. He didn't answer but looked disappointed and went away without referring to my symphonic fragment again'.

Thus, the chance of artistic collaboration between these two masters of musical showmanship was lost for ever. Berlioz completed his *Harold*, first performed about a year later by Christian Urhan, while Niccolo bestirred himself and composed a *Sonata per Gran' Viola*, with orchestral accompaniment, which he performed in London in April '34. It is a theme – rather a good one – and a set of variations so difficult in places, because of the harmonics and exceptionally high register on the top string, that one isn't surprised to hear *The Times* criticising the execution of the upper notes for being 'less clear and flexible' than on the violin. 'Altogether (*The Times* concludes) the repetition of the experiment is not what a strict regard to Paganini's fame would recommend. The violin does all that the viola can do that is worth hearing, and it does more. Paganini is unrivalled on that instrument and must remain so . . .'

Some listeners to-day might agree with that severe verdict; others would say that the development of the large viola by Lionel Tertis and the extension of its repertoire by Paul Hindemith, William Walton and Béla Bartók have amply justified Paganini's brave attempt to popularize it a century earlier. Perhaps, after all, the instrument is less well suited for virtuoso brilliance than for dreamy melancholy and if so, Paganini made a serious mistake in refusing to adapt his style to fit the delightful music Berlioz intended to write for him; *Harold* has remained in the repertoire and is held in affectionate regard by violists while the Paganini work is very rarely played, although there is an excellent performance of it available on record (see Discography, p. 164). If Niccolo felt any remorse about his dismissal of Berlioz's viola piece or any pangs of conscience about his refusal to play in Paris at Berlioz's benefit concert for distressed English Actors (including his fiancée, Harriet Smithson) he very gallantly made up for it a few years later. He was present at the first performance of *Benvenuto Cellini* in September 1838, which Berlioz later described as 'that terrible first night', and at the concert on 16th December when both the *Harold* and *Fantastic* Symphonies were performed, after which he came round with his son, Achilles, to congratulate the composer with warm effusive enthusiasm. Two days later he sent Achilles to Berlioz, who was in bed with bronchitis, to deliver a letter which read as follows: –

My dear friend,

    Beethoven being dead, only Berlioz can make him live again; and I who have heard your divine compositions, so worthy of your genius, humbly beg you to accept, as a token of my homage, twenty thousand francs, which Baron de Rothschild will remit to you on your presenting the enclosed.

    Believe me ever your most affectionate friend,

Niccolo Paganini.

Hector Berlioz, who began composing his symphony, "Harold in Italy", for Paganini but the latter refused it when he discovered too many rests in the solo viola part.

The effect on Berlioz of this exceptionally handsome present was dramatic; he was able to pay off his debts and was sufficiently free from financial worry to devote himself to the composition of one of his greatest works, the *Romeo and Juliet* Symphony. The gift, which is unique in the published history of one artist's relationship with another, received wide publicity because at that time both Berlioz and Paganini were at the centre of the Parisian journalists' reportage; it was even suggested, and believed by many, that Paganini was not the true donor but acted as a cover for another, but this calumny, which was certainly deliberate, has now finally been disproved beyond doubt.* Niccolo had made a gesture which eclipsed totally the comparatively petty misunderstandings of the past; for the remaining few months of his life he was Berlioz's *pauvre chèr grand ami*, the greatest benefactor of his career.

We must return now to the final stages – and the saddest – of Niccolo's European tour. The year 1834 began ominously for him in Paris: his illness there during the winter was diagnosed as pulmonary tuberculosis and although he recovered sufficiently to make plans for a Spring tour of Belgian cities followed by another visit to England, he realised how precariously his future career was balanced; a bad cold or an emotional upset could prevent him from playing for weeks or even months. As if this wasn't bad enough, fate played him some more unkind tricks at the same time: his violin – the faithful Guarnerius – was damaged in an accident and had to be repaired by Vuillaume (an operation watched by the owner with feverish anxiety**), and just before setting out for Belgium he injured the third finger of his left hand while cutting some cheese, an accident which made it impossible for him to practise before giving his first concert in Amiens. After two more engagements closely following each other, he appeared in Brussels, in an exhausted state, to give three concerts in one week. The orchestra was poor and under-rehearsed (he refused to employ it for the first concert and had piano accompaniment instead) and the English singers (Miss Watson and Miss Wells) went down badly with the public. The tour, completed by appearances in Antwerp, Ghent, and Bruges, was a financial success but one is left with the impression that Niccolo was beginning to find the strain of constant travel intolerable, with the result that he treated his audiences with diminishing respect. On the question of practice, for example, there's no doubt that in the earlier part of his European tour Niccolo prepared his performances with great care (he may have

---

*See de Courcy, *Op. Cit.* II p. 289.

**Vuillaume made a copy of this violin which Paganini later sold (see Chapter V). The original instrument was bequeathed to the city of Genoa where it may be found in the Sala Rossa of the Palazzo Tursi, via Garibaldi 9.

said he never practised but this boast should be treated with the same disbelief as it has been when other great solo artists have repeated it); in the later stages, however, there was little time and even less inclination to prepare. The Belgian critic, Fétis, who was so kind to Niccolo in most of his notices, shrewdly remarked in one of them that 'repose is sometimes necessary to the greatest of artists' and that 'the too active exploitation of a fine talent can only be harmful'. It was a warning which Niccolo should have heeded but back he went with the Watson troupe to London in April and immediately plunged into six poorly attended concerts on six consecutive evenings, arranged by Watson with typical lack of consideration for the artist. A short tour of the provinces, taking in Gloucester and Liverpool, was disastrous because of Watson's inefficient and parsimomious promotion, and on their return to London in May Watson was arrested for debt, having failed to pay off the orchestra for the previous month's London concerts.

The Palazzo Tursi, Genoa, where Paganini's violin may be seen.

Niccolo, evidently staggered and indignant at the public's lack of interest and the critic's lack of understanding, bailed him out and made two final appearances in the capital, the last one – on June 17th at the Victoria Theatre – being a benefit for Charlotte Watson. He left London four days later, never to return. How sad that the last experience of the world's greatest musical capital by "Europe's most spectacular virtuoso" (to borrow Miss de Courcy's phrase) should have been so atrocious!

But the moment we sympathize unreservedly with Paganini his machiavellian side seems to round upon us and we find our sympathy turns sour. The Watson affair, which now reached its climax, is an example of this. Before leaving London, Niccolo had arranged a complicated elopement for Watson's daughter, Charlotte, whom he was to meet three days after his arrival at Boulogne. All went according to plan until Charlotte stepped off the boat at the French resort which was then at the height of its season and full of English visitors. But instead of falling into the arms of her 'lover', if that is the right description for Niccolo in this case, she encountered her father, who had been tipped off about the plot and who now ensured that the press and *les visiteurs Anglais* were given a full and prejudiced account of this 'sensational scandal'. The now familiar events followed their usual course: Paganini's name was libelled in the newspapers (English as well as French), he replied with letters protesting his innocence and

When Charlotte Watson stepped off the boat at Boulogne, expecting to elope with Paganini, she found her father, accompanied by the police, waiting for her.

The engraving below shows English travellers at Boulogne.

slandering Watson, the parties then made a rapid settlement of their differences, and within a month the irrepressible Don Juan was proposing marriage to the daughter and indemnity to the father. It leaves one breathless and slightly sick. Perhaps Charlotte really was his 'devoted pupil' and he was her 'honest and dis-interested' teacher, protecting her from a 'disorderly and depraved household' and promising her 'a brilliant future'. But if so, it seems extraordinary that with all his experience Niccolo should have acted so rashly and, once again, played into the hands of his enemies.

The fact that he had enemies, who were no doubt motivated by jealousy, was harshly brought home to him when he arrived in Paris in September, having frittered away three months – and a good many thousand francs – at the casinos and other places of entertainment in Boulogne. Although he wanted to remain incognito, he was soon recognized and immediately attacked in the press (Jules Janin in the *Journal des Debats*) for failing to play for a charity. The Watsons had now departed from his life (to America, where Charlotte married three years later) so he had no concert-manager;

Some writers for the press have exercised great power over events and people, none more so than Jules Janin, pictured here in 1851, whose articles in the "Journal des Débats" caused Paganini great anguish at the end of his European tour.

114

he was feeling ill, nervous and depressed; he was anxious to get home, take possession of his country-house, and legitimize his son. With all this on his mind and physically exhausted by his travels, it's not surprising that a charity-concert wasn't at the top of his list of priorities at that moment. But here he was in Paris, the most celebrated of European artists, and here was a charity (the coal-miners of St. Etienne) which the critic, Janin, favoured and which other artists supported: if Paganini didn't jump to it and play when he was told, nothing was too bad for him. Such is the price of fame in public entertainment. Again he was pilloried in the newspapers; again he whined and cried out with righteous indignation, protesting his innocence; again he crept away, tail between his legs, this time to try and find solace at home.

On September 28th, 1834, he left Paris for Genoa, six and a half years after he had set out for Vienna. The tour which had begun with such hopes and had reached such unparallelled heights of success ended with enduring fame but with many scars and incurable illness. A conquest of Europe it certainly was but the rewards it had brought, and deserved, couldn't buy health or even reasonable happiness.

5 The End of the Road

The last five and a half years of Paganini's life were, in a sense, a retrospection of his former days, since they contained so many incidents – a mixture of tragedy and comedy – which originated in earlier events and which are all coloured by the now familiar kaleidoscope so characteristic of the man. Until nearly the end, wild enthusiasm jostled with deep depression, extraordinary generosity vied with avarice, dignity and strength of mind alternated with

A modern photograph of the Villa Gaione, near Parma, which was bought for Paganini's retirement. Reproduced by kind permission of the Parma Commune.

Vienna 1828
Giuseppe Lang modellò

Parigi 1831
A. Bovy modellò

Genova 1834
Ferraris incise
(Milano, raccolta del comm. Stefano Johnson)

When Paganini returned home to Genoa after his European tour, the city authorities struck a special medal in his honour. This civic laurel had already been accorded to him by Vienna and Paris.

pettiness and false pride; we can sympathise one moment with his hurt feelings only to be repelled the next by his lack of consideration for others, be impressed by his courage and imagination only to be saddened by his lack of common sense and sound judgement. If the first fifty odd years of his life were more than usually eventful, the last few were no less colourful; as in one of his showpieces for the violin, Paganini made the virtuoso technique predominate in his life until he had no breath left in his poor emaciated body to perform it. His light went out, as he would have wished, with more of a shout than a sigh, *con brio* rather than *perdendo*, strangulated though it was at the end.

The first important event on his return home from the European tour was the occupation of his *delizia*, the property near Parma which Germi had purchased on his behalf while he was away. The Villa Gaione was in those days evidently quite a large estate, including the three-storey house, stables, barns, vineyards, olive-groves, gardens, and adjoining land with cottages. Unfortunately, the property was already heavily mortgaged and in buying the free-hold Germi also saddled his friend with all the liabilities, an error which, as a lawyer, he should have known how to avoid. Consequently, although Niccolo appears to have tried his best to play the part of the squire and to interest himself in his tenants and dependents, his efforts to settle there and live in contented retirement were frustrated by financial wrangling and domestic discomforts; the place was too unwieldy and too much of an administrative burden for one whose business-sense was confined to the theatre box-office and who had no understanding of domestic affairs. Besides, he was temperamentally quite unsuited for the life of a placid farmer.

He was soon rushing back home to Genoa to give concerts and to be immensely gratified by his tumultuous reception and by the award of a special medal struck in his honour by the municipal authorities. But he wanted to do something helpful with his art and with the fortune he had made abroad; there was a compulsive – and very praiseworthy – strain of philanthropy in his character which was so often overshadowed by his contrary disposition to strike back at his 'enemies' that it's as well to give some examples of it now.

First, as regards money, he made a very handsome gift soon after his return to Germi of 50,000 lire 'not as recompense, but in token of my gratitude and my affectionate friendship'. True, his friend had earned it, judging by the flood of demanding letters he had received from all over Europe, and his commissions were by no means at an end now that Niccolo had reappeared, but the spontaneous generosity of the present and the obvious gratitude which accompanied it make up for a lot. His final will, which he

117

made two years later, is also notable for the liberality it accords to members of his family and former friends, not all of whom had shown a similar benevolence towards him; his two sisters, for example, were to receive the interest from separate trust funds of considerable size (75,000 and 50,000 lire respectively), the capital to revert to their children when they died (he was already contributing towards their education). Paganini's magnificent gift to Berloiz has already been described but there are many examples of small acts of kindness during these last years which are as noteworthy for the humanity which prompted them as for the actions themselves. One instance is the great trouble he took to ensure that when he sold the copy of his Guarnerius, which Vuillaume had made for him (see p. 111, note), a few months before he died, the proceeds were sent to the maker in circumstances which would not offend him.* Another small example of his basically kind nature is contained in a letter he wrote to Germi from Marseilles in January, 1837: excusing himself from coming to give a concert in Turin immediately – which infuriated Germi because he knew he was playing on the French Riviera – he asks his friend to compose for him a draft letter of

---

*See De Courcy *Op. Cit.* II p. 312.

Paganini's basically kind nature is exemplified in this letter, which thanks the recipient for looking after Achilles while his father was toruing the British Isles in 1831/32. According to the catalogue of the British Library, by whose permission the letter is reproduced, it was addressed to "Mr. G. Walters" but according to de Courcy, Op. Cit. II 33n., Achille's tutor in Paris during his father's eleven months absence was a "Monsieur G. Wolters of 4 Rue Taitbout".

thanks, in French, to the people who had helped him in Marseilles, 'famous musical amateurs', adding 'you know how very appreciative I am and that I'm not always able to express it'.

As regards his art, there is ample evidence to show that Paganini was anxious to bequeath it to posterity and to help others meanwhile to benefit from the wealth of experience he had gained abroad. For example, he made it clear in several of his letters that he wanted to publish his own works, 'and to add an explanation showing how to achieve this or that particular execution'. True, he had always been extremely careful to safeguard his compositions from 'pirates' when he was touring (not surprisingly, in view of the laxity of the copyright laws at the time) and this gave the false impression that he was too mean to allow his 'secrets' to be divulged to others. It appears probable that during his lifetime the only works for strings which reached the public in print, properly authenticated, were those published by G. Ricordi of Milan in 1820. All the other manuscripts were inherited by his son and some of them were published posthumously. In recent years one or two previously unknown manuscripts (e.g. the *Concerto in E Minor*, numbered Six, and said to be an authentic early work) have been discovered in Italy.* But although he often spoke about writing a violin-method, or 'school' as they call it in Germany, nothing of this kind appears to have survived; the fact that he was still talking about it a few months before he died seems to prove conclusively that he never accomplished it.

The most direct way in which he could have passed on his art was, of course, by teaching. Unfortunately, this seems to have been the one thing connected with the violin that he could not do. The only pupil of his who achieved any fame or recognition was Camillo Sivori, born in Genoa in 1815. Paganini gave him some lessons when he was a young boy of seven and boasted to Schottky that he had 'performed a miracle', teaching him the rudiments in a few days, and claiming that after a fortnight he was good enough to play in public. Sivori's account of his lessons, however, is less complimentary to his professor: after describing him as 'probably the worst teacher of the violin who ever lived', he narrates how Paganini used to walk about the room while he tried to play the exercises Niccolo had scribbled out for him and after he had failed to please, the demanding teacher would seize the violin and play the piece, still striding around the room, in a way which filled him with despair; the one thing he learnt, he concludes, was never to neglect practising scales. Despite this depressing experience, Sivori continued his studies under different teachers, recommended by

---

*The history of Paganini's MSS from the year of his death up to 1957 is given in Appendix IV of De Courcy, *Op. Cit.*

Paganini, and at the age of twelve was good enough to make his début in Turin; the following year he appeared in Paris and London, where he was very popular, and went on to make world tours. As his name is often linked with Paganini's because of his similar style and the ease with which he overcame technical difficulties, if would be pleasant to attribute his success to the Maestro; but from the evidence it seems clear that Sivori possessed a great natural talent which Paganini may certainly have encouraged by example but failed to perfect by tuition.

The only other pupil whom Paganini acknowledged by name — though many claimed him as their teacher — was Gaetano Ciandelli, a 'cellist. He was a mature player when he began taking lessons with the Maestro in Naples, and Paganini claimed that 'at the beginning his playing was torture to the ears and he used the bow like a novice . . . so I showed him my discovery, which produced such a great effect that in three days he was a different person and the sudden change in his playing was pronounced a miracle'. In this instance there is no record of what the pupil thought of the master but as Ciandelli himself later became a

Paganini's decision to submit himself to the demands of another "august sovereign", after his previous unhappy experience in Lucca, was a strange one. Perhaps the personality of Archduchess Marie Louise, Napoleon's second wife — pictured here — was strong enough to enveigle him once again into court circles.

120

teacher we must assume that he passed on Paganini's 'secret' (of which more later) to his own pupils.

There are no indications that once he had taken possession of the Villa Gaione he made any attempt to establish himself in nearby Parma as a professor of the violin, as his distinguished Italian predecessors had done at other places in the previous century, and as he could surely have easily done with his famous reputation. Instead, he allowed himself to be tempted by an opportunity which arose at that time to fulfil a long cherished ambition, namely, to organize and direct a fully professional orchestra. It is this curious and unhappy episode in his life that we must now examine briefly.

Although Parma in 1835 was a comparatively minor city, it was the centre of a small Duchy granted under the generous terms of the Treaty of Vienna twenty years earlier to Napoleon's second wife, the Archduchess Marie Louise of Austria. Paganini, as the titled squire of an estate within the borders of the Duchy, lost no time in presenting his compliments to his 'august sovereign', as he sycophantically described her, and in letting it be known that he was willing to place his services, in an artistic capacity, at Her Majesty's disposal. Nothing further need have resulted from this but for two chance circumstances: first, the Archduchess was anxious to re-organize the Court orchestra and to re-establish Parma as a cultural centre, and second, she was supported in this ambition by an influential but impecunious courtier, Count Stefan Sanvitale, who happened to have recently borrowed a large sum of money from Niccolo. The result of this combination of factors can easily be imagined: Niccolo became enmeshed once again in the dangerous and devious workings of a petty European court. It's inconceivable that he could have forgotten the Lucca experience; he must have believed that the royal instruction which he now had – to re-organize the orchestra and lick it into shape – would give him the independent power which he had lacked under Princess Elise. It wasn't very long before he was disillusioned.

Hurling himself into the job with customary exuberance – he forgot, temporarily, his bad health – he soon set the Court humming. The first concert he produced (including the Overtures to *William Tell* and *Fidelio*) caused, in his own words, 'a furore'. Marie Louise awarded him the Order of Constantiniano di San Georgio. His letters to Germi were ecstatic – a welcome change, no doubt from the dismal moans about his health, although his friend was rightly sceptical about the whole arrangement – and he was soon telling him that the Plan for Reorganization was nearly ready. A small cloud then appeared on the horizon. Sanvitale, alarmed at the furious speed and the likely cost of the Maestro's efforts, and aware that if he exceeded the Ducal budget it would be reported to Vienna by the Archduchess' consort (a pious and powerful one-eyed

121

blonde with the splendid name of Bombelles), told Niccolo, gently, that his commission was restricted solely to the Ducal Theatre and therefore he had no authority over Court music in general. The warning was a shock but its effect was only temporary. Had not Her Majesty's official decree given Baron Paganini exclusive charge of the music? Did it not conclude with the words: 'Tout ce que proposera Paganini sera adopté'? On with the Plan, then, and to the devil with caution!

Up to this point in the story (and I'm aware that it sounds more like the plot of a comic opera than a true history) the Parmanese musicians at the centre of the drama appear to have been carried along uncomplainingly by the tidal wave of their director's enthusiasm. But they were less content when a number of their colleagues were dismissed for inefficiency and their animosity was fully roused - with encouragement from outraged courtiers – when Niccolo engaged and fixed the salary of an outsider as orchestral leader, an appointment which belonged exclusively to the Archduchess after a competitive examination. The fat was now really in the fire. Everyone at the little Court, including the head of it, appears to have turned against this extravagant upstart Paganini, who had nearly killed himself in his efforts to raise the standard of music above that of all the other Italian cities and whose only serious mistake had been to proceed by too rapid and too straightforward methods. The Reorganization Plan was forgotten; all attempts to revive it were met with stony silence; Sanvitale was smooth but immovable (Niccolo called him perfidious, a *carogna*); a new orchestral leader was appointed from Bologna, without examination and without Niccolo being consulted. Curtain!

What was the constructive outcome of this absurd charade? It was, undoubtedly, Paganini's Plan of Reorganization for the Parma orchestra which never, unfortunately, saw the light of day but which was the most far-seeing and revolutionary conception of the modern orchestra to emerge from Italy during his lifetime. To appreciate the extent and the importance of Paganini's scheme, it is necessary to glance briefly at the state of orchestral playing in Italy at this period.

The Italians, as we have seen, were primarily interested in opera; orchestral music, *per se*, meant very little to them. Adam Carse has estimated[*] that during the first half of the nineteenth century there were between 150 and 200 theatres in Italy, most of them capable of producing opera. Until the advent of Rossini, and later Verdi, the orchestras of these theatres were accustomed to only the simplest accompaniments and were totally incapable of playing a symphony, least of all a symphony by Beethoven, even if they had been given

---

[*]Adam Carse, *The Orchestra from Beethoven to Berlioz* Broude, New York, 1949 p. 268.

Portrait favored by Paganini and often given as a gift

Portrait of Paganini in his twenty-first year

the opportunity (it is interesting that even in Vienna there was no regular professional orchestra, until very nearly the middle of the century, capable of performing symphonies by the great composers who had lived there). In Paris, London, Berlin, Dresden, Frankfurt and other German cities, Paganini had heard concert-orchestras – as opposed to theatre-orchestras, although occasionally some musicians were common to both – playing the Symphonies of Haydn, Mozart and Beethoven with a skill and polish undreamed of in Italy. In Frankfurt he had worked closely for several months with Carl Guhr, the orchestral director there, whose rigid discipline and strict attention to musical detail made a deep impression on him (as it did also on Berlioz and Wagner). In Paris he had heard Beethoven's Fifth played by the incomparable Société des Concerts orchestra under François Habeneck. In Berlin he had overcome initial hostility with the help of Gasparo Spontini and Giacomo Meyerbeer, whose consecutive rule as general musical directors covered a total of nearly thirty years, a period of brilliant musical accomplishment in the German capital. So it is not surprising to find in Paganini's Plan a provision that the Parma orchestra should give twelve subscription concerts a year and that the Music Director should have a voice in the selection of the programmes in order that they should be well balanced and artistically acceptable. He made it clear that the standard aimed at should be high – 'the works of the great masters, including the symphonies of Beethoven'.

But it would have been fruitless to set such high and unprecedented standards for an Italian orchestra without attending to certain details of organization and discipline which he had observed abroad and which he found totally neglected and out of date in Parma. The most important of these may be summarised as follows: –

> 1. Administration
> 2. The Conductor
> 3. Discipline

The administration of the Parma orchestra, when Paganini arrived on the scene, was a dichotomy – one committee looked after the finances while the other, likewise composed of court officials, dictated on the artistic side. The orchestra comprised 34 players (all professionals), with 16 probationers, a generous total compared with other court orchestras but the distribution was typically weighted in favour of the bass-line (e.g. two cellos, but four double basses) and other departments were similarly unbalanced (e.g. 3 horns, 2 trumpets, 1 trombone). The Reorganization Plan provided that the Music Director should be in sole charge of the orchestra, responsible only to the Grand Chamberlain, thus cutting out interference by a multitude of ignorant courtiers; and the orchestra

123

was to be enlarged to about 50 players, with each section musically balanced.

At the beginning of the nineteenth century the orchestral conductor, as we know him to-day, was undiscovered. Control of an instrumental piece (so far as it existed) was generally exercised jointly by the keyboard director (often the composer) and the violin-leader. This dual control inevitably caused confusion: –

The Italian orchestras are in a far from admirable condition. Lack of precision, of unity and co-operation, even lack of technical skill are noticeable everywhere ... When the violinist-leader gives the sign to begin, he strikes several times with all his might the brass candleholder of his desk, without giving the musicians the slightest hint beforehand. He then immediately draws his bow for the first stroke of the symphony, quite unconcerned whether all the rest, or only a few – or in fact anyone at all – begin with him at the same time. (George Sievers, writing in 1824 about conditions in Rome.)

Another complaint (made by Otto Nicolai, the German composer-conductor) was that even when they had started, the leader's habit of stamping his foot to keep time made more noise than the music itself.

Paganini wrote that, 'In all the important foreign orchestras there is a conductor who is so placed that he can communicate his wishes to the singers and the orchestra. He has the score in front of him on the pianoforte or conductor's desk. He stands to conduct, beats time and acts as a chronometer. The first violin is incapable of satisfactorily directing an orchestra. The only thing required of him is to be a skillful player'. And in his Plan he provided for a Court Conductor who was to receive his orders direct from the Music Director and was required to 'perform at court as directed'. We can be sure that if the Plan had been implemented and if Niccolo had been Music Director, the conductor would have been required to perform with a baton, thus anticipating the transition in Italy by at least thirty years and very likely improving the standard of playing to a level considerably above all other Italian orchestras (it was not until 1869, for example, that the orchestra at La Scala had a conductor in this modern sense of the word*).

Finally in the matter of discipline, the Plan of Reorganization suggested many far-reaching changes which would have reduced such abuses as the following: tuning instruments during a performance (especially during an opera), moving about the orchestra-pit when not playing, unpunctuality, absenteeism, failing to keep in practice, negligence in looking after instruments. And in several other disciplinary respects the Plan anticipated changes

---

*Adam Carse, *Op. Cit.* p. 316.

This bust of Paganini, sculpted in marble by Paolo Oliveri in 1835, remained for many years in the garden of his former patron, Marquess di Negro, where this photograph was taken. A recent visit failed to discover it there and it may be lying shattered in the laurel bushes, as were several other similar busts of famous Italians.

which, in some professional orchestras, have not been made until quite recently, for example, the right of the conductor to interchange desks and to refuse to accept substitutes without prior agreement. The Plan was not by any means all on the side of authority, for example, the musicians could not be punished by arrest (in Parma the Chief of Police was a member of the administrative committee!) but instead they were to be fined for mis-demeanors and the money thus collected was used for the benefit of music at the Court.

From this brief outline of Paganini's Plan in comparison with existing conditions it can be seen that his ideas were far in advance of his contemporaries'. No doubt he attempted the reorganization

125

too quickly and in the wrong way but had he succeeded, his name would have earned a distinguished place in the history of orchestral development in the nineteenth century.

Not surprisingly, the Parma episode had a profoundly depressing effect on Niccolo's morale and on his already poor health. 'It snowed this morning,' he wrote to Germi in May. 'There was ice at Gaione. For me this is the eighth month of winter – all that's lacking is an earthquake and may God send it'. And the following month he wrote, 'I have to take my medicine every day . . . It takes at least five spoonfuls of purgative . . . to obtain the necessary number of evacuations, and that's why I take the emetic every day . . . This evening, however, I don't feel like taking the second dose, as I'm too down from the first one this morning'. He was referring to the Leroy Cure which he had been taking, on and off, for about ten years and which was based on the theory that purging was the answer to all ailments. It had a disastrously weakening effect on Paganini and accounted a good deal for his emaciated condition. The combination of that and the recent blow to his pride had significant results also for his music. 'My violin is still a little out of humour with me,' he wrote, after giving three concerts in Nice at the end of the year. The awareness that his remarkable reserves of strength could no longer be relied upon to generate the 'electricity' which he needed to perform his 'miracles' on the violin must have come as a profound shock to the system. As he said himself, 'I'm glad that I've taken up my instrument again and have presented myself before the public, because such a shock has had no little effect upon my health'. He realised that his virtuoso days were over; but how could he exist without the challenge and excitement of public appearances, and of what value was his fortune if he couldn't go on adding to it? Playing the Beethoven quartets with his friends in Marseilles was a delightful pastime – always his favourite one, in fact – but it wasn't living, it wasn't dynamic. His spirit still yearned for the big occasion, the dazzling of an incredulous audience, the tumultuous applause, the flattery of Princesses and statesmen; but his physique was unable to match his courage.

Anxiety about the legacy for Achilles which he had striven so hard to accumulate, but which he was unable to pass on until his son was legitimized, led him at last to return to Genoa and to the long-suffering Germi. There he found that all the legal procedure was finally settled and he could make Achilles his legatee with his mind at rest. Perhaps this was the moment when he should have been content to settle down and 'cultivate his garden'. Instead, he went off to Turin to give two concerts and it was there that he entered into a business arrangement with his old friend and former companion, Lazzaro Rebizzo (see Chapter IV). This smooth operator – there is no other expression which adequately conveys his mixture of charm and chicanery – had conceived, with two promoters in Paris, the plan of opening a gambling casino there which would also rival the popular musical entertainments currently provided by Jullien at the Jardin Turc and by Musard at the Salle Valentino. But in order to compete with these two emperors of Parisian light music they had to acquire a name and a personality of at least equal renown and swagger. Who better than Paganini? Although forgotten in Paris now, it wouldn't be long before he drew in the crowds again with his magic bow, and his notoriety alone would entice the inquisitive public away from the extrovert Jullien. Not only that: Rebizzo, who was himself short of money, knew all about the Paganini 'millions' and was also well aware of his friend's weakness for gambling. What more appropriate establishment in which to persuade him to invest some of his huge fortune?

Once again the fates (or circumstances if one is more prosaic) combined to enveigle the impressionable Maestro into a situation where he had to be the loser. Although, on the face of it, the venture appeared promising, a little investigation and careful thought would have warned him of its dangers, even bearing in mind that it's easier to see these pit-falls in hindsight than at the time. But no, he had already agreed as early as July, 1836, to take up shares in the enterprise (see his letter to Germi, quoted by De Courcy, *Op. Cit.* II p. 239) and when he met Rebizzo in Turin the following year he was easily persuaded to keep his word. Like all good scoundrels, Rebizzo was aided and abetted by a woman – his wife – who not only persuaded Niccolo to increase his own stake to 30 shares (at 1,000 francs per share) but also to pay for an equal number for her husband who thus became a co-founder and director of the 'Casino Paganini'.

The project now being launched, the directors (there were five, excluding Paganini and Rebizzo) had to decide on the building they required and the entertainment they were going to provide in it. The site they chose was a large house in the Chaussée d'Antin (now demolished) which could be adapted to provide 'a ballroom, concert hall, billiard, gaming, and reading rooms, a retiring room, or boudoir, padded in flannel for the artists and a special armchair on the stage for the soloist, all strictly in accordance with Paganini's instructions, even to his name on the facade in gold letters two feet high'.* Here already, in this grandiose idea, lay the seeds of its destruction.

The light music which Musard and, in an even more fantastical way, Jullien were providing in Paris was intended not for the

_____

*De Courcy, *Op. Cit.* II p. 257.

A note in Paganini's own hand to his friend Germi, sending him some variations, about which, he says, words fail him. "Signora Camilla" was Germi's mistress, Camilla Beretti, with whom he lived for many years before they were eventually married in 1837.

serious-minded but, as Adam Carse says in his fascinating *Life of Jullien*, 'for the masses of ordinary Parisians who walked about the boulevards and sat down in the gardens and restaurants or went to a theatre for their evening's amusement'. The quadrilles, Overtures, gallops, waltzes, marches and *tableaux vivans* which they put over with such inimitable flair and panache, to a background of laughter, chatter, and tinkling of glasses, were a far cry from Paganini's conception of a kind of Arts Centre, catering for the cultured minority, combined with a gambling establishment for the exclusively wealthy. The Casino would certainly have failed as a rival to 'Napoleon Musard', even if its principal drawing powers had been allowed to function as intended.

But they were not allowed to function. First, Niccolo was so ill by this time that he was unable to do more than make a brief appearance at the opening ceremony and thereafter, according to Berlioz, to take an occasional walk round the grounds when the weather was fine. Secondly, at the very same time as the Casino was due to open, Johann Strauss and his Viennese orchestra began a three week season in Paris and attracted great crowds. Thirdly – and perhaps most disastrously – the municipal authorities refused a gambling licence. Consequently, after a few weeks of desultory business over the Christmas period, the whole scheme collapsed like a pack of cards. Worse was to follow.

The Casino was ordered by the city authorities to close early in the new year because it had infringed the law in engaging the chorus from the Opéra as a substitute for Paganini. The directors, insolvent and owing money in all directions, sued him for 100,000 francs damages, claiming that he had failed to honour an agreement to play. Rebizzo, inevitably, left Paris in a hurry and

Louis Jullien, the great showman of Parisian light music in the 1830's. The "Casino Paganini" could not have survived as a rival to the Jardin Turc, even if its star performer had been well enough to appear.

A Paris lithograph of Paganini at the time of the Casino disaster. He was so ill that he had to move into a sanatorium for the treatment of chronic illness.

refused to answer requests for the return of the 30,000 francs which Niccolo had paid up for his shares. The fiasco of the Casino left a trail of lawsuits, anger and bad feeling which would have been enough to depress its chief victim even if he had been in the best of health. But, in fact, Niccolo was very ill indeed and had moved from his quarters at the Casino to a private sanatorium for the treatment of chronic illness. He wrote from there to Germi, 'Some day Rebizzo will be sorry that he treated me so barbarously. He's the cause of all my woes'. One feels some sympathy with this view, certainly, but most of his troubles in this episode could have been avoided if he had taken sensible precautions and it was unfair to blame Rebizzo for everything.

Throughout that Spring and Summer of 1838 Germi continued to receive dejected letters; they were mostly concerned with doctors, medicines, the abominable climate, promises of wonderful cures, descriptions of his painful efforts to follow prescriptions and diets. But punctuating these tales of misery were signs of all his old humour, courage, and hope. For example, a letter in which he complains that the doctors in Paris are no good and that he is tormented every night by pains in his thighs and legs, by fever and coughing, promises that when he returns to Italy he will bring 'Beethoven's last quartets, which I should love to play for you, as well as those of Spohr'. In another he says that he hasn't slept for twelve days because of the fever, pain and cough, but refers also to the 'three big sonatas' he's composed, one of which (does he mean *La Primavera – The Spring*?) is 'worthy of the Queen'. The Queen of England, perhaps? He had recently spoken of planning a short visit to London and of telling the English that he wanted to dedicate the last of his music to them. By September he says he is feeling a

130

little better and even talks of visiting Russia (in mid-winter!) and by the end of the year he is pestering Germi once again to recover his debt from Rebizzo.

Yet in spite of all the 'slings and arrows of outrageous fortune' which he had had to endure this year, it was in December that he made his munificent gift to Berlioz (see Chapter IV). He felt, perhaps, that in saving a budding genius from extinction he was salvaging what he could from his own sinking vessel and investing it in the art which meant everything to him. If this sounds a naïve explanation of Paganini's famous gesture, at least it fits with what he had already tried and failed to achieve himself in Parma and in Paris – a memorial to his own musical gifts. Berlioz himself certainly interpreted the gift in this way, recognizing that he now held in trust, as it were, part of the Italian's artistic legacy. 'I always hoped to see him return to Paris', he wrote, after Paganini's death. 'I waited until the symphony (i.e. *Romeo and Juliet*) was entirely finished and printed before sending it to him and meanwhile he died at Nice, leaving me – together with so many other sad regrets – that of not knowing whether he would have considered worthy of him the work composed chiefly to please him . . . He, too, seemed to feel a very real regret in not knowing "Romeo and Juliet" and wrote to me in that vein in his letter of January 7th, 1840, from Nice, saying, "Now that everything is finished, envy must be silent". Poor dear good friend!' Whatever the incredulous detractors (Hallé and Liszt among them) said about the gift, it is comforting to know that Berlioz recognized his benefactor's well-intentioned motive.

Niccolo finally got away from Paris on a freezing cold Christmas night (he chose some odd times to travel) and arrived at his old friend Camille Brun's house near Marseilles ten days later. He was lucky to have this refuge; the house was evidently comfortable and his host, a dealer in musical instruments, was able to raise his spirits by encouraging him to join in playing chamber music and by reviving his interest in composition. The idea also occurred to Niccolo that it would be no bad thing for his depleted finances if he poached on the buying and selling of instruments, provided he traded through middle-men, because, he was shrewd enough to realise, if people knew that Paganini wanted to buy a violin they would double the price! This new interest livened him up considerably and he was soon forgetting some of his troubles, writing round to all his contacts in various countries and regaining a lot of his old enthusiasm. Some of these letters make very interesting reading because they throw extra light on his own choice of instruments, strings and bows during his heyday; they also reveal his almost superhuman courage – to lose one fortune and within six months plan to make another, in spite of mortal illness!

On Christmas night, 1838, Paganini left Paris for Marseilles, a sick and broken man. Shortly before departing he sat for this portrait by de Pommeyrac. Paganini is wearing the Order of the Austrian Royal Household medal ("Der Tugend") – see page 10 – a rather pathetic reminder of former glories.

Niccolo's favourite violin was said to be his Guarnerius del Gesu of 1742 (known as the 'cannon'), bequeathed by him to the city of Genoa and now at the Palazzo Tursi Via Garibaldi. (see page 112). This may have been the instrument given to him by M. Livron in Leghorn when he was a young man (see Chapter I). He carried it around Europe in a battered old trunk but experience must have taught him to have more respect for these beautiful examples of the old makers because at the end of his life he cherished them as treasures and, like many dealers, he was reluctant to part with them even for good money. He realised also the value of a good bow but seems to have had very decided views about their construction and tension for his own use. For example, in a letter written to Germi in 1832 he explains that he requires 'more hairs' than the average bow possessed and 'maximum elasticity'; this no doubt contributed to the speed and clarity of his up-bow staccato, which was described by one critic as 'rapid, thrilling, little louder than a whisper, but of such a wizard awfulness that it makes you shiver'. Fétis, more objectively, wrote that Paganini's bow was of ordinary dimensions but the hair was tightened with more than usual tension and that his 'bounding staccato' differed from that of other violinists for this reason. When he was asked to try out a steel bow which Vuillaume had invented he wrote a highly appreciative letter of commendation, although, according to one report he added: 'As far as my experience goes, the merits of a bow are infinitesimal – the only difference lies with the player'.[*] If that is an authentic remark, it sums up Paganini's attitude to the art of bowing very neatly. The dimensions of the strings he used have caused a lot of controversy because some critics accused him of breaking them on purpose in order to show off his ability to perform difficult music on fewer than four strings. Paganini didn't discourage this fallacy and it may be true that the thin gut which he used at the peak of his career broke more often than the thicker variety which had been popular with his predecessors. The purity of tone, which was a feature of his playing, and the clarity required for the harmonics could only be obtained from thin strings; conversely, the plucked accompaniments with the left hand – another feature – placed a great strain on them and he was one of the first great violinists to appreciate the added strength of a new invention – a string wound with silver thread.

His vast experience of giving concerts under great pressure in many different types of hall and in varieties of climate placed him in a special position to judge the potentialities of instruments, bows and strings; his knowledge of the science of violin-playing had not been acquired from books but from practical experience 'in the

---

[*]Quoted by de Courcy, *Op. Cit.* II p. 176.

Sketch depicting Paganini's dramatic feat of performing works solely on the G string

Paganini's violin in the Municipal Palace at Genoa

field'. If his violin required adjustment or minor repair when he was touring in the remoter parts of Europe, there was no one to undertake it but himself. But when he visited any town where a luthier worked he called in to chat, exchange information, and examine the instruments available. So it's not surprising that his letters about violins written in the last year of his life contain evidence of detailed practical knowledge and wise advice. For example, '. . . don't talk to me of repaired violins with visible cracks; but negotiate for good violins of strong wood that hasn't yielded at the bridge. And let's leave all the other defective instruments to the dealers. For instance, the Amati violin I received from you will be very difficult to sell because the sounding board is too damaged and also because Amatis haven't a high standing . . . Therefore, try to get me the most beautiful Strad and Guarneri cellos, violas, and violins, as above, since I want to succeed as a dealer in stringed instruments'.

The 22 instruments listed in Appendix V of de Courcy as being in Paganini's possession at the time of his death may give some indication of his activity as a dealer during the Spring and Summer of 1839 but it's impossible to say how successful he was in terms of money or reputation. One can only guess that he found it difficult to trade effectively by remote control from such a distance but at least it provided him with an outlet for his frustrations and an occupation during long hours of enforced idleness, for his health showed a steady deterioration during these months, in spite of his frantic recourse to any doctor or specialist who showed the slightest interest in his condition, and by September, when he left Marseilles for Genoa (by boat!), he was unable to stand upright without help. He had already heard that all the efforts of Germi in Italy and of his lawyers in Paris to defend the suit for damages and to recover Rebizzo's debt had been in vain. The damages, personal loss, and legal fees resulting from the Casino venture amounted in all to about 160,000 francs. There is no record, apparently, of the damages ever being settled but the worry of it and the irritation of knowing that he had been duped and grossly maligned hurt him more than the financial disaster itself. His friends at home were appalled by the advanced state of his illness and begged him to stay among them but, convinced that the damp winter mists falling from the mountains upon Genoa were bad for his loss of of voice and wretched immobility, he left for Nice (again by boat!) after a few weeks. It was to be his last journey.

No description of Niccolo's final struggle with adversity can adequately convey the pathos and tragedy of a man who had reached the pinnacles of artistic and material success but who was now reduced to a lonely and loveless decline in a foreign environment. True, he had occasional visits from friends and letters

133

from home (Achilles was with him but appears to have left no account of his father's last days) but the sun which he sought at Nice rarely entered his life again, either in reality or metaphorically. Some would say that this was just retribution for a profligate and a sinner, particularly as he refused – on the grounds of physical inability – to receive the local parish priest who wanted, prematurely as it turned out, to administer the Last Rites. This was naturally held against him by the Roman Church after his death and was one of the chief causes of his posthumous notoriety as we shall see. Niccolo seemed as incapable of observing the conventions of death as those of life. He didn't want to die; he clung desperately to any vestige of hope proffered by any doctor, whether practising or not; linctus for catarrh, poultices for rheumatism, purgatives followed by sedatives for the stomach – all of these and many other 'remedies' were followed until they proved to be ineffective, until at last he cried out, 'Great God, I have no more strength'.

In April he was still dictating letters to Germi about the Rebizzo debt, refusing any suggested compromise, and when urged to forget

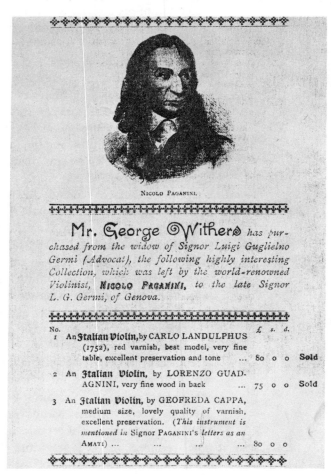

NICOLO PAGANINI.

Mr. George Withers *has purchased from the widow of Signor Luigi Guglielmo Germi (Advocat), the following highly interesting Collection, which was left by the world-renowned Violinist,* NICOLO PAGANINI, *to the late Signor L. G. Germi, of Genova.*

No.		£	s.	d.	
1	An Italian Violin, by CARLO LANDULPHUS (1752), red varnish, best model, very fine table, excellent preservation and tone	80	0	0	**Sold**
2	An Italian Violin, by LORENZO GUADAGNINI, very fine wood in back	75	0	0	Sold
3	An Italian Violin, by GEOFREDA CAPPA, medium size, lovely quality of varnish, excellent preservation. (*This instrument is mentioned in* Signor PAGANINI's *letters as an* AMATI)	80	0	0	

Paganini collected many fine stringed instruments, especially during the last few years of his life. When he died, some of them were acquired by his friend Germi whose widow evidently sold them – with other Paganini relics – through George Withers & Co., London, as this interesting catalogue shows.

134

No. | | £ | s. | d. |
---

4 A superb **Italian Alto**, by HIERONYMUS AMATI, large size (uncut), very perfect preservation, covered with very beautiful red varnish; most magnificent tone. (*This instrument is mentioned in the letter No. 22*)... 200 0 0

5 An **Italian Violoncello**, by RUGERIUS, medium size, very perfect preservation ... 400 0 0 Sold

6 An **Italian Guitar**, by GENNARO FABRICATOR, Anno 1819, Napoli; ebony ornamentation over table. (*This instrument was for many years used by* NICOLO PAGANINI)... 25 0 0

7 A large **Oil Painting of Nicolo Paganini**, taken from life by J. BULWER. (*This is considered the best likeness in existence*) ... 50 0 0 Sold

8 A **Marble Bust**, 24 inches high, reputed to be by CANOVA, who was an intimate friend of PAGANINI'S ... 50 0 0 Sold

9 A ditto, in plaster ... 10 0 0

10 A **Manuscript Quartett** for Violin, Alto, Violoncello, and Guitar. Unpublished. By NICOLO PAGANINI. No. 10. (*These Quartetts are mentioned in several of the letters, and were written for Signor Germi*) 4 4 0

11 A ditto. No. 11 ... 4 4 0

12 A ditto. No. 12 ... 4 4 0

13 A ditto. No. 13 ... 4 4 0

14 A ditto. No. 14 ... 4 4 0

14A A ditto. No. 15 ... 4 4 0

(Nos. 10–14A: Sold)

15 An **Original Letter**, in SIGNOR NICOLO PAGANINI'S own writing, to his Advocate, LUIGI GERMI, dated Dec. 20th, 1835 ... 4 4 0

16 A ditto, June 2nd, 1815... 3 13 6 Sold

No. | | £ | s. | d. |
---

17 An **Original Letter**, in SIGNOR NICOLO PAGANINI'S own writing, to his Advocate, LUIGI GERMI, dated March 2nd, 1840 3 13 6 Sold

18 A ditto, Feb. 24th, 1819... 5 5 0

19 A ditto, Feb. 21st, 1839... 5 5 0

20 A ditto, Dec. 14th, 1833... 6 6 0 Sold

21 A ditto, Dec. 14th, 1829... 5 5 0

22 A ditto, Feb. 17th, 1834... 6 6 0 Sold

23 A ditto, Feb. 15th, 1840... 6 6 0 Sold

24 A ditto, Dec., 1818 6 6 0 Sold

25 A ditto, March 9th, 1834 5 5 0 Sold

26 An **Original Composition** (16 pages) 5 5 0 Sold

27 A small ditto ... 1 0 0 Sold

28 A ditto, an Obligato for the Viola on all four strings ... 3 3 0 Sold

29 A **Violin Bow**, silver mounted ... 4 4 0 Sold

30 An **Alto Bow**, very fine octagon stick of great strength, silver mounted ... 5 5 0 Sold

31 A **Violoncello Bow**, octagon stick 3 3 0

32 A ditto, round stick, silver mounted ... 4 4 0

the past and think of the present he replied that he didn't believe one should lose sight of the future. The spirit was unconquerable but the body had had enough. Haemorrhage followed haemorrhage and on May 27th, 1840, he died, still without absolution.

Paganini on his death-bed. The design for this lithograph is attributed to his son, Achilles.

135

6 The Paganini Legend

Before following the extraordinary events of Niccolo's post mortem adventures, it may help to be aware of the territorial and religious settlement in the north-west corner of Italy which resulted from Napoleon's defeat and exile in 1815. The settlement was very largely the work of the Austrian Chancellor, Metternich, and was therefore reactionary and repressive; Metternich wanted to stifle all vestiges of incipient Italian liberalism, which French occupation had encouraged, and all traces of nationalism which posed a threat to Austrian domination. At the same time, he wanted a strong bulwark on the western frontier with France against any military adventure which that country might contemplate in the future. Thus, he restored to its former rulers, the Kings of Sardinia, the huge territory of Piedmont, Savoy and Nice. To complete the discomforture of the Italians, he added the former Republic of Genoa.

The Genoese were strongly inclined towards liberalism and nationalism; their's had been one of the first states in Europe to welcome the tricolour; Mazzini, born in Genoa, was the founder of 'young Italy', the movement which initiated Italian unification; Genoa was the port of departure of Garibaldi and his thousand 'red-shirts', who later freed the south of Italy from the autocratic government of the *ancien régime*. It followed that Genoa disliked Metternich's settlement intensely and had little respect, at first, for their new ruler or for his hereditary dominions with which they were now linked. By choosing to die in Nice, Niccolo ensured that his liberal-nationalist compatriots practically ignored the event; he might just as well have died in Vienna.

If his place of death did nothing to endear him to the Genoese, his manner of dying was no less objectionable to the elders of his Mother Church. The settlement of 1815 had restored not only the politics of repression in Italy but the full authority of an old fashioned Pope. Backed up by the Inquisition, the Index (prohibiting unorthodox literature), and the Jesuits, ecclesiastical matters were once again dominated by those medieval methods – spying, extortion, intolerance, and the rigorous persecution of heretics – which had brought so much misery in the past. Reforms under Pope Pious IX came too late for Niccolo who died not only without absolution but, perhaps more important,

"The body was embalmed and left for two months on his death-bed". This was only the start of Paganini's post-mortem adventures.

without including the Church as a beneficiary in his will.

So it's not surprising that when news of his death reached Genoa the civic authorities showed little interest (to their way of thinking he had died 'abroad'), and when the local priest told the Bishop of Nice scandalous stories about his refusal to fulfill his Easter duties and to receive absolution, the Bishop decreed that he couldn't be buried in consecrated ground.

The family and friends – Achilles and Count de Cessole were mainly responsible – tried desperately to have the decision reversed. An ecclesiastical court was set up but this only made matters worse: wild stories and gossip were eagerly told to the investigators by Niccolo's detractors, chiefly his maid whom he had sacked just before his death. The body was embalmed (an early example of this) and left for two months on his death-bed; then it was removed to the cellar of the house where it remained for over a year. Meanwhile, his friends in Genoa tried to obtain permission to bring him back home; it was refused. Germi sent a petition to the King who was more sympathetic but could do nothing without the Church's approval and the Church remained obdurate; Paganini, they said, had lived a wicked life and had died impenitent, forgetting he was a Christian. If anyone was forgetting Christian morality and teaching, it seemed to be the Church!

There was but one course left – an appeal to the Pope. Achilles, accompanied by a Genoese lawyer (Germi was himself too ill to go) set off in September, 1841, for Rome. While they were there the health authorities in Nice ordered the body to be removed from the cellar. De Cessole – one imagines he was at his wit's end by this time – took it to an abandoned leper-house on the rocky coast near Villefranche where it was dumped in the corner of a damp and gloomy cell. Soon the stories began to circulate: weird and terrifying noises were heard by fishermen passing the place at dusk; the strains of a violin, said others, could be distinctly identified

137

While Paganini's family and friends were trying to arrange for his body to be sent back to Genoa, another friend in Nice was forced by the local authorities to move it from place to place in secrecy.

from across the water on a calm evening; unearthly signals emanating from the building were felt by holidaymakers climbing over the rocks. Poor de Cessole! Even his money couldn't buy the silence of helpers he had to trust. Once again he was forced to move the unwelcome corpse, first to the cement vat of an olive-oil factory, then – suitably at midnight – to the garden of a private house on the promontory of Cap Ferrat.

At last, in April, 1844, very nearly four years after death, the body of Niccolo Paganini encased in three coffins (there had been a cholera epidemic on the French Riviera and de Cessole was taking no more chances) was transported by ship to Genoa and from there by wagon to his family's house at Raimarone, the country place where, as a youth, he had helped to plant vegetables.

Achilles had succeeded eventually in obtaining permission for his father to land at his home port but his Church still refused to receive him. A year later (April, 1845) he obtained permission from Archduchess Marie Louise (Paganini's former patroness) for the body to be transferred to the Villa Gaione, where it was interred in the garden, but it was not until 1876 that the iniquitous verdict of the Bishop of Nice was rescinded and the remains were transferred to the cemetery in Parma. In 1893, the Czech violinist, Franz Ondricek, persuaded Achille's son, Attila, to allow the coffin to be exhumed so that he could see the corpse – a macabre episode which most of us would call revolting but which would probably have appealed, ironically, to Niccolo himself. A further exhumation occurred three years later, when a new cemetery was opened at Parma; one of the viewers wrote that 'Paganini's features were still recognizable but . . . the lower part of the body was nothing but a heap of bones'.* A large monument was erected over his final grave by the family and the main epitaph reads:–

Here lie the remains of Niccolo Paganini,
A violinist who inspired the whole of Europe
By his divine music and supreme talent,
Conferring great and unprecedented renown upon Italy.

One cannot read about the post mortem affairs of Paganini without feeling some degree of indignation with the bigoted attitude of the ecclesiastical authorities. True, he had failed at the end to abide by the doctrines of his Church; refusing the sacrament at Eastertide, refusing confession and absolution before death were serious offences. True, he had lived a dissolute life and there appeared to be little evidence of any penitence or willingness to reform. True, he had a reputation for meanness, in spite of his great wealth, and the Church did not benefit from his will. But if these transgressions amounted to a formidable indictment, surely there was much to be said on the other side? He was desperately ill when he arrived in Nice and the local priest was tactless to call without preliminary introduction. His sinful life was balanced by the pleasure he had given with his music. His avarice was mitigated, as we have seen, by many individual acts of kindness. But above all, the Church was wrong to pass judgement on a dead man; Paganini had never been excommunicated, he had been baptised by the Church and he remained, officially, a member of the Roman Catholic church until the day he died. To judge the condition of his soul after death and to condemn it was no less of a heresy than those for which they condemned him.

The only valid excuse one can fabricate for the obstinate and unbroken silence of the authorities in response to the pleas of Paganini's family and friends for him to be given a Catholic burial is that during their investigations they stumbled upon evidence of a sin which was too awful to reveal. We have seen how the satanic association, which Paganini made fun of when talking about it with friends, rebounded on him unfavourably in later life. It seems just possible that the curia, determined to probe every corner of Paganini's private and public life, discovered evidence which, in their view, substantiated the wild stories of his devilish relationship. There was certainly no lack of rumour on the subject and if it seems incredible that intelligent people took it seriously one has only to remember the powerful effect of any psychological phenomenon upon pious and unworldly minds. Such a discovery, with its terrible and unspeakable connotations, would at least

*I am indebted to De Courcy (*Op. Cit.* Ch. XXXVII) for the factual details of Paganini's several interments.

139

explain why there was never any recorded reply from Rome to Achille's petition. It would have been impossible for an honest reply to be given without levelling a charge which could never be substantiated and which would have appeared ludicrous to the materialist.

That Paganini did possess a strong psychical force, however, has become an undoubted part of the legend which began to build up around him after his death and this has been given various shades of meaning and significance by different writers.

In a well known nineteenth century book, *The Violin* (the following quotation is from the fifth edition of 1878) George Dubourg wrote:

Paganini's existence was a series of alternations between excitement and exhaustion; and it is not surprising to find that his moods were variable and uneven, and that he would sometimes sit, for hours together, in a sealed and sombre taciturnity, whilst, at other times, he would surrender himself to a wild effervescence of gaiety, without any apparent motive in either case.

The story that Paganini had perfected his talent while undergoing a long term of imprisonment for murder was common gossip in many of the cities he visited and although he laughed it off initially it caused him great indignation later. This original drawing by John Ruarke would have been lithographed eagerly by all the print-shops of Europe's main cities from 1828 onwards.

Artistic attempt to capture moods of Paganini

H. R. Haweis

Stendhal (1783-1842)

Taking the same point but investing it with a deeper significance, the Rev. H. R. Haweis (*My Musical Life* 1884) wrote:–

What made Paganini so exceptionally great was the portentous development, the strength and independence of the emotional fountain within. The whole of life was to him nothing but so many successions of psychological heat and cold. Incidents immediately became clothed with a psychic atmosphere – perhaps the life of emotion was never so completely realised in itself, and for itself, as in the soul-isolation of Paganini. That life, as far as it could be individually expressed, was uttered forth by his violin.

All great artists depend upon a fund of emotion which, allied to technique, makes them what they are. Paganini's emotion was so closely bound up with his own psyche that its potency fluctuated, according to his mood, more widely than is normal. This is the reason why some of his performances made an unforgetable impression upon audiences, while others were much less memorable; it also accounts for his occasional references to the 'electricity' (there is no other translation of his word *eletricismo*) which he considered it was necessary to generate for a good performance. When musicians in Europe took stock of his achievement after 1840 they naturally fastened on this psychical power as a feature and it became an important aspect of the Paganini legend.

The darker side of his personality, especially his alleged imprisonment for murder, became entangled with the psychic aspect of the legend. Passing reference has been made to the story, which began circulation in Italy at about the time of his Milan début, that Paganini had perfected his talent while undergoing a long term of imprisonment for murdering his mistress (some versions substituted her husband as the victim). When he first heard about it, Niccolo laughed it off and was probably rather pleased, at that time, with the additional publicity it gave him. Later, in Rome, he was shocked and angry to see it repeated in print by Stendhall (Henri Beyle) in his *Life of Rossini*, a work which was neither authentic nor honest, even about its subject. During his European tour the story cropped up again in Vienna, Paris, London and many other cities with unfailing regularity; he was haunted by it. But it was no longer a joke. His success as a free-lance virtuoso now depended upon the support of royalty, the aristocracy, the highly placed; it would not do to be caricatured as an ex-gaol-bird. Moreover, there were some sections of the press, especially in Paris, which used the story maliciously, with the intention of denigrating the Italian 'invasion' of the artistic world; Paganini was represented as a serious menace to the 'purity' of violin-playing as exemplified in the French style. This so much alarmed him that he asked Fétis to write the letter, published over his signature in the *Revue Musicale* and dated April 21st, 1831, which was given wide publicity and which has always been regarded as Paganini's definitive answer to the calumny of his imprisonment.

SIR, – So many proofs of kindness have been showered upon me by the French public, so much encouraging approbation has been bestowed upon me, that I cannot avoid believing in the fame which it is said preceded me in Paris, and that I fell not short of my reputation at my concerts. But, if any doubt of that kind existed in my bosom, it would be removed by the eagerness evinced by your artists to produce my likeness, and by the great number of portraits of Paganini – faithful resemblances or not – which cover the walls of your city; but, sir, it is not only simple portraits that speculators of that nature stop at – for, while walking yesterday on the Boulevard des Italiens, I saw in a shop, where engravings are sold, a lithograph representing Paganini in prison. 'Oh!' I exclaimed, 'here are some honest folks who, after the fashion of Basile, make a profit out of certain calumnies which have pursued me for the last fifteen years'.

However, I examined laughingly this mystification, with all the details that the imagination of the artist had conjured up, when I perceived that a large number of persons had congregated around me, each of whom, confronting my face with that of the young man represented in the lithograph, verified the change that had taken place in my person since my detention. I then saw that it was looked on in a serious light by those you call, I believe, louts, and that the speculation was a good one. It struck me that, as everybody must live, I might furnish the artists, who are kind enough to consider me worthy of their attention, with some anecdotes – anecdotes from which they could derive subjects of similar facetiæ to the subject in question. It is to give them publicity, that I claim from your kindness the insertion of this letter in the 'Revue Musicale'.

They have represented me in prison; but they are ignorant of the cause of my incarceration; however, they know as much of that as I do myself, and those who concocted the anecdote. There are many stories in reference to this, which would supply them with as many subjects for their pencils; for example, it is stated that, having found a rival in my mistress' apartment, I stabbed him honourably in the back, while he was unable to defend himself. Others assert, in the madness of jealousy, I slew my mistress; but they do not state how I effected my bloody purpose. Some assert I used a dagger – others that, desirous of witnessing her agony, I used poison. Each has settled it in accordance with his own fancy. Why should not lithographers have the same privilege? I will relate what occurred to me at Padua, nearly fifteen years since. I had played at a concert with great success. The next day, seated at the table d'hôte (I was the sixtieth) my entrance in the room passed unobserved. One of the guests spoke of the great effect I had produced the previous evening. His neighbour concurred in all that was said, and added, 'There is nothing surprising in Paganini's performance – he acquired his talent while confined in a dungeon during eight years, having only his Violin to soften the rigours of his confinement. He was condemned for having, coward-like, stabbed one of my friends, who was his rival'. As you may imagine, every one was shocked by the enormity of my crime. I then addressed myself to the person who was so well acquainted with my history, and requested to know when and where this had taken place. Every eye was directed towards me. Judge the

Paganini in prison, lithograph by Louis Boulanger

S. Barth's interpretation of Paganini's prison days

surprise when they recognised the principal actor in this tragical history! The narrator was embarrassed. It was no longer his friend who had been assassinated. He heard – it had been affirmed – he believed; but it was not improbable he had been deceived. This is how an artist's reputation is trifled with, because indolent people will never comprehend that one may study at liberty as well as under lock and key.

My mind was disturbed for a long time by these reports, and I sought every means to prove their absurdity. I remarked that from the age of fourteen, I had continued to give concerts, consequently was always before the public; that I had been engaged as leader of the orchestra, and musical director to the Court of Lucca; that if it were true, I had been detained eight years in prison, for having assassinated my mistress or my rival, it must have taken place before my appearance in public; that I must have a mistress and a rival at seven years of age. At Vienna I appealed to the ambassador of my country, who declared he had known me for upwards of twenty years as an honest man, and I succeeded in setting the calumny aside temporarily; but there are always some remains, and I was not surprised to find them here. How am I to act, sir? I see nothing but resignation, and submit to the malignity which exerts itself at my expense. I deem it, however, a duty, before I conclude, to communicate to you an anecdote, which gave rise to the injurious reports propagated against me. A violinist, of the name of Duranowski, who was at Milan in 1798, connected himself with two persons of disreputable character, and was induced to accompany them to a village, where they purposed assassinating the priest, who was reported to be very rich. Fortunately, the heart of one failed him at the moment of the dreadful deed, and he immediately denounced his accomplices. The gendarmerie soon arrived on the spot, and took Duranowski and his companion prisoners at the moment they arrived at the priest's house. They were condemned to the galleys for twenty years, and thrown into a dungeon; but General Menou, after he became Governor of Milan, restored Duranowski to liberty, after two years' detention. Will you credit it? – upon this groundwork they have constructed my history. It was necessary that the violinist should end in 'i', it was Paganini; the assassination became that of my mistress or my rival; and I it was who was sent to prison, – with this exception, that I was to discover there a new school for the Violin; the irons were not adjudged against me, in order that my arms might be at perfect liberty. Since these reports are persisted in, against all probability, I must necessarily bear them with resignation. One hope remains: it is, that after my death, calumny will abandon its prey, and that those who have so cruelly avenged my triumphs, will leave my ashes at rest.

PAGANINI

The last sentence seems prophetic, as well as pathetic. For many years after his death the stories about his imprisonment continued and, until quite recently at least, were accepted as part of the Paganini legend.

If the label 'ex-convict' was used dishonourably by his detractors, the epithet 'avaricious' was employed with no less venom and, perhaps, with a little more justification. It originated in his practice (from about 1820 onwards) of doubling the normal price of tickets for his concerts, at home and abroad, and of demanding at least two-

143

Paris le 16 novembre 1832

Mon cher Laporte,

J'ai reçu votre aimable lettre du 9 courant, et je suis bien sensible au désir que vous m'y exprimez de m'avoir pour la saison prochaine, ainsi qu'aux propositions que vous me faites à ce sujet; mais comme je me propose de faire un grand voyage dans le midi de la France, et même de retourner pour quelque tems dans ma patrie, où mes affaires m'appellent, je ne saurais me retourner à Londres l'an prochain, et d'autant moins que j'ai déjà dit à plusieurs Anglais, que je n'y reviendrais qu'en 1834. Ce sera donc vers cette époque, que je vous écrirai, pour pouvoir nous arranger ensemble.

Je viens d'apprendre par Mr Séguin, que vous êtes en négociation avec Mme Eckerlin; je crois dans votre intérêt, que cet artiste distingué, que j'ai eu occasion...

thirds of the receipts for himself and his assistants, the pretext being that his performance was much above the average entertainment usually provided. We have seen that in London this immodest and grasping attitude was greatly resented but in some other cities in England Paganini's 'double or I quit' régime was accepted for precisely the reason that he himself believed in, as the following extract from the *York Herald* shows: –

144

In conclusion, it is perhaps only an act of justice briefly to advert to the many unfavourable reports put in circulation respecting Signor Paganini, most of which, if not all, have their origin in that littleness of mind which envies talents it cannot reach. Rapacity, exhorbitance, and avariciousness, are charges that have been plentifully heaped upon him, besides others of a worse description. Many of the stories thus told, bear their refutation in the fact, that Signor Paganini cannot speak one word of English, and all his pecuniary affairs are managed by his Secretary. Through this deficiency, he may also have been led into mistakes, but it is hardly possible that a mind like his, so full of soul and sensibility, whose whole life has been a sacrifice to severe application in his profession, can be so devoted to narrow feelings and mean extortion as he has been represented to be. One thing, however, is certain, he has given unmixed satisfaction to all who have heard him in York, and he has opened a new field for future violinists, so that in a few years we may hope to witness wonderful effects from his labours, the fruits of which will be reaped long after he is no more. He has given us a performance unparalleled in the history of music, and our citizens have not been much imposed upon, at all events, since, with all the extra attractions of the Concerts, only three shillings more than the usual prices were required.

Without doubt Paganini did exploit his talent more selfishly than his contemporaries (Chopin, for example, made two public appearances in Vienna, the year after Paganini's visit, for no payment at all) and he was never willing to perform 'gratis', however distinguished the company or however deserving the cause, unless he had volunteered to do so himself. Such reluctance to be imposed upon is now understandable because it is accepted that a professional musician should be paid the fee he can command; but it was not understood at all in the nineteenth century when musicians, even the top ones, had barely emerged from a position of servitude. Indeed, the most remarkable fact about Paganini's attitude is that for most of the time he got away with it. That it gave him an unenviable reputation for avarice, which stuck to him after his death, would probably in his view have been a small price to set against the great wealth he amassed and against the principle, which he helped to establish, that a great artist should be suitably rewarded for his services in money. He received many pieces of jewellery, gold medals and snuff-boxes during his travels, from crowned heads and wealthy admirers, but, although he sometimes mentioned these gifts proudly in letters to Germi, he mentioned the box-office receipts much more often.

Even on the question of money, however, there is something to be said in Paganini's favour. He was often prepared to play in very small theatres or halls in out of the way places where the receipts barely covered his costs and one can't imagine many international soloists who would do that in modern times. Until his bad health got the better of him, he was usually conscientious about not disappointing his public and any exhibition of genuine enthusiasm

at one of his concerts would often persuade him to give another in the same town, however crowded his schedule. This often led him into trouble because a second appearance in a small place, arranged on the spur of the moment, was poorly attended and the promoters, finding themselves badly out of pocket, tried to bargain with him to reduce his fee; on these occasions he was always adamant in his refusal and in the ensuing rows he would pursue his claim, however small the sum involved, with the determination of a Shylock. In circumstances of this kind, when he was on the defensive and protecting what he considered his rights, he was at his worst – petty, mean, undignified. But when he was welcomed as an

One reason why Paganini's concerts in London were poorly attended in 1832 was the counter-excitement caused by the Parliamentary Reform Bill. This picture shows the Duke of Wellington, who thought that the English people were very quiet if they were left alone, being mobbed at the height of the frenzy. The King finally gave his assent to the Bill shortly before Paganini's first concert.

146

outstanding artist, treated as a man of honour, and applauded for his feats—as in Edinburgh, for example—he returned the compliment with charm and generosity. In the Scottish capital there was no hesitation on his part in agreeing immediately to a request from the Lord Provost to give a charity concert (on November 16th, 1831), although it involved some inconvenience. But a few months later *The Harmonicon*, the leading British musical journal of the day, castigated him for giving a charity concert in Paris in aid of the cholera victims, saying that 'he gave no concert for charity purposes here!' Miss de Courcy points out (*Op. Cit.* II, p. 78) that this lie was repeated in print as recently as 1946, which indicates how Paganini's unjust reputation for invariable cupidity lingered on long after all the trifling arguments had been forgotten.

In any assessment of this extraordinary man's character the matter of his health and physique must feature prominently; sporadic illness accounted for many of the characteristics for which he is often remembered and his remarkable prowess on the violin has often been attributed by posterity to abnormalities in his physical structure. That Paganini suffered chronic illness of some kind from about the age of thirty seems to be certain; what is not known—and probably never will be—is the nature of the disease or to what extent it was exacerbated by his succession of treatments, some prescribed by leading European doctors, others picked up by the suffering patient from any quack who sympathised. Dr. Francesco Bennati, an eminent physician and a specialist on ailments of the larynx, was also a musician and his personal friendship with Paganini probably began in Italy. In 1831 Bennati published, in Paris, a long paper (*Histoire physiologique et pathologique de Niccolo Paganini*) which he had previously read to the French Academy of Sciences and in which he broadly attributed the violinist's emaciated condition and recurring bouts of fever to neurasthenia, tracing its origins to his childhood attacks of measles and scarlet fever and to his hypersensitive skin. He emphatically denied that Paganini had tuberculosis and referred only indirectly to the syphilitic condition which had long ago been diagnosed and which some opinions linked with laryingeal phthysis. Moreover, he ignored the treatment which the patient had been receiving for this condition. In about 1822 Paganini had first consulted Dr. Sira Borda, a University professor in Pavia, who had diagnosed syphilis and prescribed a course of mercury and opium, to be applied both internally and externally. The results—stomach ulcers and rotting gums—were not fully apparent until Bennati examined him in Vienna six years later; by that time the patient had had all his bottom teeth removed and had undergone an operation to remove infected bone from the lower jaw—an unenviable experience, to put it mildly.

147

But such was Paganini's inner strength and determination that he continued a variety of treatments: he wore dark glasses in artificial light in order to save his eyes, visited German spas to drink the waters, followed homeopathic courses recommended by their inventor, Dr. Hahnemann, and continued with a strong emetic and purgative ('Leroy's Cure') whenever he felt it necessary. He had become a hypochondriac by the time he arrived in London, spending hours shut up in his room and refusing to see anyone, but the stimulus of a concert was usually enough – almost incredible as it seems – to rouse him from his depression and afterwards the excitement of success carried him on its shoulders for a few days or weeks until he sank into another trough. *The Times* account of his first London concert (June 3rd, 1831) was nearer the truth than its author may have realised in this paragraph: –

Another major factor in the depletion of Paganini's audiences on his second visit to London was the cholera epidemic which began in England at the end of 1831 and soon spread to London. Poor housing and a contaminated water supply contributed to the spread of disease. This general view of London in 1830 gives some idea of the cramped urban conditions, although Paganini and Achilles were lucky in renting a house near Regent's Park.

There is a singularity in his manner, which though partaking of the grotesque, denotes a man of no ordinary stamp, and rivets attention in a very extraordinary degree. The interest which he excited was a good deal increased by his appearing to be in a very weak state of health. Indeed, up to a late hour in the day, it was doubtful, we understand, whether he would be able to perform; and his appearance altogether is said to have been contrary to the judgement of his medical advisers.

Certainly, a man of 'no ordinary stamp' who could galvanize himself to concert-pitch from a state of wretched depression and then give a performance fit to cause an uproar of enthusiasm. If all his critics from this time onwards had been shrewd enough to

148

observe, or kind enough to discover, his actual state of health, they would not have been as short of understanding as they often were; even Janin, in Paris, couldn't have been mean enough to slash at the reputation of a man whose courage exceeded anything a reasonably healthy person could ever conceive.

But the stories were told and the legend was born: Paganini was unsociable, taciturn, unpredictable, he looked crooked, wild-eyed, distraught; his manners were slip-shod, his clothes disreputable, his personality uncouth. In a book published in London in 1955, the author wrote: –

. . . there (in the Hanover Square Rooms) the terrible, weird man, Paganini, with his flashing eyes, his long hair streaming over his shoulders, his cadaverous face and gaunt limbs, has, with his bony, lissom fingers, extorted such exquisitely beautiful, such passionate, such eloquent yet such wild and half-distraught strains from his violin, that, hearing him, you might have imagined him as one struggling with an evil spirit, whom he had imprisoned in his instrument, and who was frantically striving to burst his bonds.*

Thus, the image has been passed down to us. But with the knowledge we now have about his health, some of his seeming faults become positive virtues and it's amazing that he was able to carry on such an active life for so long. The secret of his long battle against the odds lay in his often-repeated phrase, 'the philosophy of the violin', for he had made the violin correspond, in his person, to the ultimate reality of life itself. In becoming the master as well as the slave of the violin, he discovered more knowledge of it than he ever discovered of life or of other people. Of him it can be truly said that the Child became father of the Man.

Did Paganini ever try to pass on his 'secret' to others, or did it perish – as Fétis believed – encapsulated in those much-travelled coffins, with him? He told Schottky that 'only one single solitary person' knew his secret and that person was Ciandelli, the cellist who was for a time his pupil (see Chapter V). If that was true, it seems surprising that during his last years, when he realised the seriousness of his illness, he didn't impart the mysterious information to someone else who would be certain to publicize it. The Frankfurt musician Carl Guhr made a conscientious and methodical attempt to analyse Paganini's playing and to note what he did differently from other violinists, namely: the tuning (scordatura), the bowing (the bounding staccato is particularly noted), the low height of the bridge (thus facilitating the execution of chords), the use of harmonics (the thin strings made these easier to produce), his preference for the G string, and finally, his special

*From *The Old Concert Rooms of London* by Robert Elkin, Edward Arnold, London, 1955, p. 104.

effects (such as the combination of bowing with left-hand pizzicato). Some of Guhr's observations were confirmed by other writers; Fétis, for example, agreed that Paganini's method of fingering bore no resemblance to the one usually taught. But one feature which seemed to defeat analysis by Guhr or anyone else was the violinist's posture, the way he held the instrument and the bow. Cartoonists always showed him in the shape of an elongated triangle, with his elbows almost touching, and there is ample evidence that constant practice in youth caused his left shoulder to be at least an inch higher than the other, even in repose. The exceptionally high arch of the right wrist was another characteristic frequently caught by the artists and this may have accounted for the elasticity of his bowing and for the comparatively thin tone, a matter which attracted the attention of several critics in different countries. But the question which naturally occurred to other musicians anxious to copy Paganini's skill was whether his hands were larger and more flexible than normal; if they were, there might be no need to look any further for his 'secret'. Their enquiries met with limited success – it appears that his left hand was exceptionally supple (he could bend the thumb back, without effort, 'to an extraordinary degree') and Guhr said that he could 'easily span three octaves', even with 'rather small and thin' hands. Fétis described his hands as 'large, dry, and nervous', adding that 'the thumb of the left hand fell easily upon the palm of his hand when necessary for the execution of certain shifting passages'. Dubourg quotes another contemporary observer who wrote: 'Such is the flexibility of his joints that he can throw his thumb nearly back upon his wrist and extend his little finger, at the same time, in the opposite direction. By these means, when in the first position, as it is called, of the violin, he can reach, without shifting, to the second octave. His extreme high notes – for he contrives to play three octaves on each string – are given, consequently, with a precision and certainty never heard before. This flexibility, without doubt, is indispensable to the execution of many of the passages . . .'*

These few examples are enough to show us that Paganini's contemporaries were partially misled by his use of stopped and open harmonics. When they talk of 'spanning three octaves' they mean that with the use of harmonics he could cover three octaves on each string. And it is certain that his mastery of all the harmonics which the violin can produce beguiled his listeners into thinking that the span of his left hand was much greater than it actually was. The conclusion, then, about Paganini's 'secret' is that

---

*In a paper published in *The American Medical Association Journal* (Jan. 2nd, 1978) the author, Dr. M. R. Schoenfeld, advanced the theory that Paganini suffered from – or benefited by – Marfan's syndrome.

150

Caricature of Paganini performing

Poster for concert of works by various composers

Poster for concert of Paganini's compositions

he was the first great violinist to exploit harmonic notes to the point where, in conjunction with stopped notes, they provided a new dimension *in the type of music he exclusively played in public*. The emphasis is required because for other types of music the use of harmonics, to the extent he employed them, is neither necessary nor desirable. In a violin concerto by Bach, Mozart, or Beethoven, for example, frequent use of harmonics would be out of place – indeed contrary to the style and meaning of the music. But Paganini never played these composers' works in public, in spite of very strong hints that he should. In his second English tour of 1833, for example, there was one critic in Brighton discerning enough to raise this very point. 'His auditors (he wrote) are astonished beyond measure at his wonderful facility – at the admirable rapidity with which he performs various passages, and at the unerring precision with which he introduces his harmonics; but still we believe there are few musicians who would not prefer hearing him perform a larghetto of Mozart or Beethoven in the same chaste and simple style which distinguished the first part of the last piece he performed on Monday, or the Preghiere from *Mose* which he played here last year. Paganini sometimes gives a bar or two of a slow movement but the effect is in general immediately destroyed by flying off into some capriccio. Candour compels us to admit that we do not think his tone superior, if equal to, one or two other violinists'. And in a notice of a second concert given in the same week, the critic could find no fault but this: 'There is only one thing to be desired with regard to Paganini. We should exceedingly like to hear him play an adagio movement of any great master. We can easily conceive that Paganini's reason for composing his own music is to enable him to introduce his own peculiar style, and to give scope to the exquisite skill which he possesses; in short, to execute such passages as no other man would ever think of writing. So far we fully approve of his plan; but the English public would, he may depend upon it, be still more gratified, could they hear him perform some of the compositions of established authors'.

But Paganini had been persuaded once – in Paris – to perform some compositions by 'established authors' and his notices had been exceptionally bad. Fétis summed up the position admirably: –

To pronounce judgement upon Paganini (he wrote) it was necessary to hear him in his own special style – that which most characterized his talent. In his concerts in Paris, he thought it necessary to flatter the national feeling by playing a concerto by Kreutzer and one by Rode – but he scarcely rose above mediocrity in their performance.

Fétis went on to quote Paganini's own answer to those who criticized him for playing his own works exclusively, which he had given to his secretary, George Harrys: –

151

I have my own special style and in accordance with this I formulate my composition. To play works of other artists I must adapt them to my style. I would much rather write a piece myself in which I can trust my own musical feelings entirely.

And perhaps it would be wise to allow Fétis the last word on this matter of Paganini's 'secret': –

Paganini's art did not apply to any species of composition – he was a speciality, of which he alone could be the interpreter – an art born with him, the secret of which he has carried with him to the grave . . . there is, however, something astounding and mysterious in the skill which Paganini possessed of invariably overcoming almost unheard-of difficulties . . . death has not permitted the secret, of which he spoke, to be divulged.

There was one violinist, however, who claimed to have received direct tuition on how to play Paganini's music from the composer himself – after death!

Florizel von Reuter was born in America at the end of the last century and came to Europe with his widowed mother when he was seven; he was already a prodigy on the violin and gave concerts in London and other European capitals at the age of nine, causing a sensation wherever he appeared. His performance of Paganini's music at this early age was considered particularly remarkable and he earned the nickname, 'Paganini redivivus'. At the height of his very successful career as a violin-virtuoso, when he was about thirty, he re-visited America and stayed with old friends – the Hon. and Mrs. Lyman J. Gage. Gage, who had been Secretary of the Treasury under Presidents McKinley and Roosevelt, was now an old man but he and his wife were both interested in psychic research, as well as in music, and they aroused some curiosity in Von Reuter, to the extent that he attended a scéance at the Gage's house. During that evening, when he was still very sceptical about the whole matter, he had his first contact with the spirit of Paganini, which he described as follows: – *

Florizel von Reuter, already a child prodigy on the violin when he came to Europe from America with his mother at the age of seven.

I will, in conclusion, relate one incident which was, in its way, rather phenomenal. A 'Spirit voice' was suddenly heard to remark: 'There is a great violinist present, who wishes to greet the young gentleman. He says his name is Paganini'. I therefore began to address the invisible 'Paganini' in his own language, Italian, and was surprised to receive answers in the same language. The voice was so faint that it was difficult to catch every word, but I was able through several sentences to glean that the voice was referring to my mother. An instant later the voice had floated over to my mother on the opposite side of the circle, and began to speak in her ear.

*This and following extracts are taken from *Psychical Experiences of a Musician* by Florizel von Reuter, published by Simpkin Marshall Ltd., and The Psychic Press, London, 1928, with an Introduction by Sir Arthur Conan Doyle.

152

And now comes the really remarkable part of the incident. The alleged 'spirit' began to thank my mother warmly, in fluent Italian, for having influenced me before my birth, and in my childhood, to become interested in him and his music. My mother then remarked: 'He plays all your twenty-four Caprices'. 'Yes, I know,' came the answer; 'I have often been present in concerts where he has performed them'. 'Were you contented?' asked my mother. 'Molto, molto contento' (very, very contented), replied the voice.

I then ventured to inquire if it would be possible for him to play something on my violin, which I had placed on a small table at my elbow for all eventualities.

Another 'spirit-voice' now spoke, saying: 'He will try, but as this is the first time he has got into touch with the earth-plane, it will probably be difficult'.

I took my violin and bow in my hand, and the next moment the bow disappeared from my hand and the strings of my violin were plucked by an unseen hand. A moment later I placed my right hand on the finger-board and distinctly felt something touch the back of my hand above my wrist. Soon after the bow was restored to me, the nut of the bow being placed as accurately in my hand as if put there by someone who understood how to hold a bow, and as if returned to me with a bright light in the room.

That was the end of the 'Paganini' incident.

The remarkable point is that, in truth, my mother did will me before my birth to become a violinist, taking the personality of Paganini as a model for the fulfilment of her desires, a fact which, needless to say, was unknown to everyone present except herself and me.

In the course of my career as a virtuoso I have acquired a reputation for my interpretations of Paganini's music, have repeatedly given lectures on his life, and have published a number of new editions of his works. If it be true, that the spirits still take interest in earthly matters and do follow the careers of human beings, then there would be nothing illogical in the idea that the spirit of Paganini would be attracted by such an exponent and champion of his music.

Some time later, in Germany, he came across and later acquired an apparatus called the 'Hesperus-Additor' – 'a board of polished wood about twelve inches long by five wide. Along the upper half of the long side of this board the alphabet was printed, in addition to numerals up to ten and the phrase "Greeting in the name of God". With this simple board went a peculiar little round hollow box with a pointer protruding from it . . . if one put this box, hollow side down, on the lower half of the board, turning the pointer towards the letters, and then placed the tips of one's fingers on the smooth top, the box would soon begin to move automatically and messages of the most complicated characters would be forthcoming'.

Von Reuter and his mother experimented with this apparatus for a long time before eventually receiving messages, in a simple code, which convinced them that they were in touch with a guardian-spirit. However, the renewal of contact with Paganini came much later and then not by means of the apparatus but through trance-mediums, again in America. On these occasions, Von Reuter

153

received advice, through several different mediums, about his forthcoming programmes and shortly afterwards, while practising, alone, Paganini's *La Campanella*, he experienced a curious sensation:–

Suddenly, without any premeditation, while playing a difficult passage, my fingers seemed to be impelled (I can find no other adequate expression) to abandon suddenly the fingering I had used for years, the substitution of a perfectly different fingering taking place as naturally as if it had been a simple passage instead of a very complicated one. Overjoyed at the unconscious discovery of a vastly more satisfactory fingering, I continued playing, on the alert for any more suggestions I might receive.

And sure enough, in the course of the ensuing hour, I received at least a dozen new ideas in nuancing, fingering, and bowing, the effect being as though the suggestions were given me through telepathy, or that my bow and fingers were being controlled by another Intelligence than my own.

The next day, upon playing the composition again, I found the new ideas as firmly fixed in my mind as if I had taken a lesson with some violin master, but I no longer experienced the sensation of being controlled by another personality. I have never forgotten the peculiarly distinct impression I experienced on that day, and cannot keep from feeling that Niccolo Paganini had thus begun to fulfil his intention of 'going through the programme' with me.

I will not endeavour to explain scientifically the experience. Scientists will probably say auto-suggestion or hallucination. Let the reader draw his own conclusions.

As Von Reuter points out, neither he nor his mother knew enough Italian to translate some of the words as they were received. But they continued their experiments and one day he asked 'Niccolo' (the name by which the contact always introduced himself) to give some advice while he actually played a piece of Paganini's music (*I Palpiti*). He describes what happened:–

My mother kept her hand on the Hesperus while I played and from time to time a word was written, for example: con fuoco (with fire); piu capriccioso (more capriciously); prestissimo (as quickly as possible); con piu sentimento (with more sentiment); staccato, etc. Once, to indicate a strong vibrato, the Hesperus began to tremble violently. Another time it raced madly up and down the board, in order to signify a greater acceleration of speed. Still again, the box turned on the side and jerked up and down the board as fast as possible to indicate 'staccato'. I must lay stress upon the fact that none of the words written were printed upon the music, yet they were in every sense applicable to the passage which they referred to. Now, while it is true that my mother has considerable knowledge of music, also of interpretation, having closely followed my studies and been present at the majority of my lessons when I was a small boy, yet I would certainly not credit her with the ability to give me subconsciously advice on the subject of interpretation which would be of value to me, by calling my attention to finesses which my own conscious powers of observation had overlooked.

That would be attributing to my mother's subconsciousness greater discrimination than I, an intellectual, fully developed artist, would be consciously capable of.

Yet the fact remains that upon this occasion, as well as upon several other occasions which lack of space does not permit me to refer to in detail, I have received advice upon interpretation and nuancing (expression) finesses which had not occurred to me, and certainly seemed to point to the guidance of a higher authority upon such finesses in violin interpretation.

I make this statement objectively, and without any tendency to exaggerate the importance of the advice received, because it purported to come from a higher source.

The very fact that the advice always referred to more or less trivial details renders it peculiarly convincing in my eyes, as such minor issues would only occur to an authority upon pedagogical shading.

Had the advice touched more important points, I would unhesitatingly credit my mother with the ability to ferret them out, but not such minute details as were mentioned. No one could do that save a past-master of the highest order.

Even when events and bad health were making life difficult for him, Paganini's sense of fun was never far below the surface. It seems appropriate, therefore, to include two pictures which exemplify his enjoyment of life. The first is a note, obviously written in a hurry, inviting a friend to join him in his box at Covengarden (sic.) that evening. One hopes she(?) accepted.

155

As von Reuter himself said, in another context, 'Let the reader draw his own conclusions'.

On another occasion he received from 'Niccolo' the following:—

My compositions are not Beethoven, but at least they are good for the technique. In order to remain stationary on the highest peak of art in violin-playing, one should practise every day all branches of technique, from the cantilena to the transcendental.

The von Reuters' experiments with the 'Hesperus' and 'Niccolo' included writing questions on ten slips of paper, mixing them up face down, so that neither of them knew which question was being asked, then holding up each piece of paper in turn and asking for an answer through the little box. The purpose being to eliminate any possibility of mutual telepathy between mother and son. To eight out of the ten questions the 'Hesperus' gave consequential affirmative or negative answers.

Their contact with 'Niccolo' continued, periodically, for a long time and he became their control-guide, introducing them to others—sometimes to other musicians, for example, Joachim, or sometimes to their personal friends and relatives who were dead. They even claimed to have been told about life 'on the other side'—for example,

On one occasion we asked my aunt to tell us something about how and where she lives now. She described her spirit-house as being approached by a spacious and lovely drive, the house itself being surrounded by a veranda with great flowering wisteria covering it. To our question as to how the house was kept clean, she gave the somewhat enigmatical answer: 'Night tidies everything. Holy is the night'. (Query.—Is there night in the spirit-world?) She furthermore stated that we would not be capable of understanding if she were to try to describe how beautiful her abode was. We asked her if she heard much music. She answered: 'Very much lovely music. Paganini recently gave a great concert'.

Wondering how she would get around the next question, I asked: 'What does he play on?' The answer came back: 'An old violin'.

I then asked: 'Where does he get such a violin from in the spirit world?'

I am afraid I spoke a trifle sarcastically. The answer was a great surprise to us both. 'From his thoughts. God wills that each person should have that which he most needs'.

The reason why Conan Doyle became so interested in the von Reuters was because they were put in touch with several authors—for example, Emile Zola, Joseph Conrad, Charles Dickens—one of whom, Jerome K. Jerome, he had known very well. After meeting them and observing their method with the 'Hesperus-Additor' very carefully, Sir Arthur became convinced that some of their experiences were evidential and that they were in touch with 'intelligences outside themselves', their special bond

Sketch of the Paganini bust, showing the degeneration of his face due to surgery and the removal of teeth

From the bust by Dantan

with Paganini being explained, he thought, by the view that 'those who live on a different vibration from ourselves are aware of us when our thoughts are turned to them'. Mrs. von Reuter had had a strong wish, while her son was still in her womb, that he should 'play the violin like Paganini' and it was to her that 'Niccolo' addressed his most affectionate messages, reserving the advice on technique and the interpretation of his music for her son. All the same he never revealed any fundamental secret about playing the violin to Florizel von Reuter, so on that score we are no more enlightened; perhaps he thought his 'pupil' was doing very well without it!

In the final summing-up of his first biographical sketch of Paganini, Fétis wrote: 'If any violinist can play, with perfect intonation, and in the required tempo, the passages of Paganini's concertos, he will consequently attain absolute certainty in ordinary music'. If we take this to mean that mastery of Paganini's concertos renders all other violin music relatively simple, the last hundred and fifty years have amply disproved the statement; a complete change of style has made it invalid, for a start. But if we paraphrase Fétis and say that no one but a great *stylist* can play Paganini's music, we are speaking the truth. Complete technical skill is essential, of course, but the manner of interpretation is the over-riding factor. A contemporary wrote, as early as 1818, 'His performance bears the stamp of the eccentricity of his character. His tone and the thrilling intonation of his double stops are electric. His bow moves as if it were part of himself, endued with life and feeling'. The same observation was noted by Carl Guhr. After comparing Paganini with the other great violinists of the age—Rode, Kreutzer, Baillot, Spohr—he remarked: '. . . he has opened a way peculiar to himself, which essentially separates him from those great artists; so much so that whoever hears him for the first time is astonished and transported at hearing what is so new and unexpected;—astonished by the fiend-like power with which he rules over his instrument;—transported that, with a mechanical facility which no difficulty resists, he at the same time opens to the fancy a boundless space, gives to the violin the divinest breathings of the human voice, and deeply moves the inmost feelings of the soul'.

In fact, all the commentators who tried to describe Paganini's playing refer to his depth of feeling and to the infinite variety of tone he used. It would be a great mistake to place his music in the category of 'technical fireworks' and to forget his love of opera, for on that he built the melodies, the dramatic intensity, and the puckish humour of all his works. Italian opera of the period—Rossini in particular—is the best guide to an appreciation of Paganini's style.

In his obituary notice of Paganini, Berlioz wrote that he was 'one of those artists of whom it must be said that they are because they are, not because others were before them'. Many violinists since then have brought their own individual style to the instrument and in doing so have enriched its power and its ability to enthral, to astonish, to uplift. But none has brought the violin to a new peak of excellence equal to Paganini's; his achievement is unique and perhaps it will remain so. The legend about him which we have inherited is a strange mixture, for both his personality and his artistry were flamboyant projections of an internal strength which was immeasurable. But the aim of this book will have been fulfilled if those who have read it now want to become better acquainted with Paganini's music and with the violin-world which he dominated. Some would say that his spirit still dominates that world's successors.

Paganini's later concerts, sketched from life

Bust of Paganini

Select Bibliography

Biographies

Anders, G. E. *Niccolo Paganini. Sa vie, sa personne, et quelques mots sur son secret* Paris, 1831.

Berri, Pietro *Il Calvario di Paganini* 1940.

Bonaventura, Arnaldo *Niccolo Paganini* Rome, 1911.

Codignola, Arturo *Paganini Intimo* Genoa, 1935.

Conestabile, Giancarlo *Vita di Niccolo Paganini da Genova* Perugia, 1851.

Courcy, G. I. C. de *Paganini, the Genoese* 2 vols. University of Oklahoma Press, 1957 (re-printed by Da Capo Press, New York, 1977).

Day, Lilian *Paganini of Genoa* New York, 1929.

Farga, Franz *Violins and Violinists* London, 1950
Geigen und Geiger Zurich, 1940.

Fétis, F. J. *Notice biographique sur Nicolo Paganini* Paris, 1851.

Harrys, George *Paganini in seinem gesellschaftlichen Zirkelu und seinen Konzerten* Braunschweig, 1830.

Istel, Edgar *Nicolo Paganini* Leipzig, 1919.

Kapp, Julius *Paganini* Berlin, 1913.

Laphalèque, Imbert de *Notice sur celèbre violiniste Nicolo Paganini* Paris, 1830.

Niggli, Arnold *Nicolo Paganini* Leipzig, 1882.

Prod'homme, J. G. *Paganini* Paris, 1907.

Pulver, Jeffrey *Paganini, the Romantic Virtuoso* London, 1936.

Saussine, Renée de *Paganini le magicien* Geneva, 1950.

Schottky, J. M. *Paganini's Leben und Treiben als Kunstler und als Mensch* Prague, 1830.

Sheppard, Leslie and Herbert R. Axelrod *Paganini* Paganiniana Publications, U.S.A., 1979.

Stratton, Stephen S. *Nicolo Paganini: His Life and Work* London 1907.

Tibaldi-Chiesa, Maria *Paganini. La Vita e l'opera* Milan, 1940.

Valensi, Theodore *Nicolo Paganini* Paris, 1950.

General

Abraham, Gerald *A hundred years of Music* 3rd Ed. London, 1964.

Anderson, Emily *The Letters of Mozart and Family* London, 1938; *The Letters of Ludwig van Beethoven* London 1961.

Apel, W. *Harvard Dictionary of Music* 2nd Ed. Cambridge, Mass. 1970.

Barea, Ilse *Vienna, Legend and Reality* London, 1966.

Berlioz, Hector *Memoirs* Paris, 1878 (translated and edited by David Cairns, London, 1969).

Blume, Friedrich *Classic and Romantic Music* (translated by M. D. Herter Norton) London, 1972.

Boero, G. B. *Genealogie di Niccolo Paganini* Genoa, 1940.

Bonaventura, Arnaldo *Gli autografi musicale di Paganini* Florence 1910.

Boscassi, Angelo *Il violino di Niccolo Paganini* Genoa, 1909.

Burney, Charles *A general History of Music* (London, 1776-89) 4 vols. New York, 1957.

The Present State of Music in France and Italy London, 1771 (Ed. by Percy A. Scholes, London, 1959).

The Present State of Music in Germany, the Netherlands, and United Provinces London, 1773 (Ed. by Percy A. Scholes, London, 1959).

Carse, Adam *The Orchestra from Beethoven to Berlioz* Cambridge, 1948.

Celada, I. *Paganini a Praha* Prague, 1940.

Chopin, Frédéric *Lettres Complètes* Paris, 1933.

Combarien, Jules *La Musique et la Magie* Paris, 1935.

Costa, Antonio *Il Teatro Carlo Felice 1828-1844* Genoa, 1844.

Dendelot, A. *La Société des Concerts du Conservatoire, 1828-1923* Paris, 1923.

Demuth, Norman *An Anthology of Musical Criticism* London, 1947.

Dorian, F. *The History of music in Performance* New York, 1942.

Doring, Ernest *How many Strads?* Chicago, 1945.

Einstein, Alfred *Music in the Romantic Era* New York, 1947

Elkin, Robert *The Old Concert Rooms of London* London, 1955.

Ferrari, Vittorio *Il Teatro della Scala nella vita e nell'arte dalle origini ad oggi* Milan, 1922.

Fétis, F. J. *Biographie universelle des musiciens* 8 vols. Paris, 1860-65.

Fleuriot de Langle, Vicomte Paul *Elise, Soeur de Napoléon I* Paris, 1947.

Foster, Myles B. *History of the Philharmonic Society of London, 1813-1912* London, 1912.

Grout, D. J. *A History of Western Music* New York, 1960.

A short History of Opera 2 vols. 2nd Ed. New York, 1965.

Grove, —. *Dictionary of Music and Musicians*

Hart, George *The violin: its famous makers and their imitators* London, 1872.

The Violin and its music London, 1875.

Hill, A. *The Violin-makers of the Guarneri family* London, 1931.

Hill, Ralph (Editor) *The Concerto* London, 1952.

Jacobs, A. *Music Lover's Anthology* London, 1948.

King, A. Hyatt *400 years of Music Printing* London, 1964.

Kinsky, G. *A History of Music in Pictures* London, 1937.

Laforet, Clause *La vie musicale au temps romantique* Paris, 1929.

Lahee, henry C. *Famous Violinists of To-day and Yesterday* Boston, 1916

Lang, P. H. *Music in Western Civilization* New York, 1941.

Lazzareschi, Eugenio *Il soggiorni di Paganini a Lucca* Lucca, 1940.

Liszt, Franz *Berlioz und seine Haroldsinfonie* 1855.

Locke, A. W. *Music and the Romantic Movement in France* London, 1920.

Mancini, Augusto *Storia di Lucca* Florence, 1950.

Montovani, R. *Le Secret de Paganini* Paris, 1922.

Marmottan, Paul *Les Arts en Toscane sous Napoléon. La Princess Elize* Paris, 1901.

Bonaparte et la République de Lucques Paris, 1896.

Elise Baciocchi Paris, 1898.

Marriot, Sir J. A. R. *Makers of Modern Italy* Oxford, 1931.

Masson, Frédéric *Napoléon et sa famille* Paris, 1908.

Monti, Umberto *Giancarlo di Negro* Genoa, 1950.

Moser, Andreas *Geschichte des Violonspeils* Berlin, 1923.

Nardi, Carlo *Il Lintaio Cesare Cande e il violino di Paganini* Genoa, 1949.

Nerici, Luigi *Storia della musica in Lucca* Lucca, 1878.

Neicks, Frederick *Chopin as a Man and Musician* 2 Vols. London, 1888.

Pannain, Guido *Musica a musicisti in Napoli nei secoli XIX e XX* Rome, 1923.

Papi, Egidio *Il teatro municipale di Piacenza. Cento anni di storia* Piacenza, 1912.

Passeti. *Il Teatro Communale di Ferrara* Ferrara, 1915.

Pincherle, M. *Les violinistes; compositeurs et virtuoses* Paris, 1922
  An Illustrated History of Music London, 1960.

Portales, Guy de *Berlioz et l'Europe romantique* Paris, 1939
  Franz Liszt Paris, 1926.

Roberti, Melchiorri *Milano, capitale Napoleonica* Milan, 1946.

Rodocanachi, Emmanuel *Eliza Napoléon (Baciocchi) en Italie* Paris, 1900.

Ross, Janet and Nellie Erichsen *The Story of Lucca* London, 1912.

Salzedo, S. *Paganini's Secret at Last* London, 1916.

Scholes, Percy A. *God Save the Queen* Oxford, 1954.

Schreiber, O. *Orchester und Orchesterpraxis in Deutschland 1780-1850* Berlin, 1937.

Schulze, Friedrich *Hundert Jahre Leipzig Stadttheater* Leipzig, 1917.

Sfilio, Francesco *Alta cultura di tecnica violinistica* Milan, 1937.

Singer, Kurt *Diseases of the Musical Profession* New York, 1932.

Sitwell, Sacheverell *Liszt* London, 1934.

Smart, Sir George *Leaves from the Journals of Sir George Smart* London, 1907.

Spiracke, Harold *Paganiniana* Washington DC, 1945.

Spohr, Louis *Louis Spohr's Selbstbiographie* 2 vols. Kassel, 1860-61.

Stoering, Paul *The Story of the Violin* London, New York, 1904.

Thayer, A. W. *The Life of Ludwig van Beethoven* 3 vols. Berlin 1866-79 (Latest Edition New York, 1960).

Tiersot, Julien *Hector Berlioz et la société de son temps* Paris, 1904.

Toye, Francis *Rossini* New York, 1934.

Turner, W. J. *Berlioz, the Man and his Work* London, 1934.

Vannes, René *Dictionnaire Universelle de Luthiers* Brussels, 1951.

Vatielli, F. *Arte e vita musicale a Bologna* Bologna, 1927.

Vernarelli, Gerardo *Niccolo Paganini nei disegni di un impressionista contemporaneo* Rome, 1940.

Walker, Ernest *A History of Music in England* Oxford (Ed. by J. A. Westrup), 1952.

Weissmann, Adolf *Der Virtuose* Berlin, 1920.

Westrup, Sir Jack *An Introduction to Musical History* London, 1955 (Latest Edition, 1973).

Williams, Hugh Noel *The Women Bonapartes* New York, 1909.

Wyndham, Henry S. *The annals of Covent Garden Theatre 1732-1897* London, 1906.

Yorke-Long, Alan *Music at Court* London, 1954.

Young, Percy M. *The Concert Tradition* London, 1965.

Discography

The following L.P.'s and tape-cassettes (denoted by TC followed by the number) are generally available from dealers in Great Britain:—

Concertos Nos. 1–6 for violin and orch.
    Accordo, LPO, Dutoit 2740-121, TC 3378-067
Concerto No. 1 (E flat)
    Ricci, LSO, Collins ECS 654
    Menuhin, RPO Erede ASD 440
    Ashkenasi, VSO, Esser 2535-207, TC 3335-207
    Perlman, RPO, Foster SLS 832
    Perlman, RPO, Foster ASD 2782
    Campoli, LSO, Gamba SPA 183
    Hasson, New Phil, Devos CFP 40052
    Accardo, LPO, Dutoit 2530-714, TC 3300-714
    Szering, LSO, Gibson 9500-069
    Belkin, Israel PO, Mehta SLX 6798, TC KSXC 6798
    Ishikawa, Prague CO, Kosler 110-2076
Concerto No. 2 (Bm)
    Ricci, LSO, Collins ECS 654
    Menuhin, RPO, Erede ASD 440
    Ashkenasi, VSO, Esser 2535-207, TC 3335-207
    Accardo, LPO, Dutoit 2530-900, TC 3300-900
Concerto No. 3 (E)
    Accardo, LPO, Dutoit 2530-629
    Szering, LSO, Gibson TC 7300-103
Concerto No. 4 (Dm)
    Szering, LSO, Gibson 9500-069
Concerto No. 5 (Am)
    Accardo, LPO, Dutoit 2530-961
Concerto No. 6 (Em)
    Accardo, LPO, Dutoit 2530-467
Introduction and Variations on a theme from Rossini's 'Cenerentola' ('non più mesta)
    Accardo, LPO, Dutoit 2530-900
    Accardo, LPO, Dutoit TC 3300-900
Maestoso Sonata Sentimentale (Variations on Austrian National Anthem)
    Accardo, LPO, Dutoit 2536-376, TC 3336-376
    Accardo, LPO, Dutoit 2530-961
    Accardo, LPO, Dutoit TC 3300-900
I Palpiti
    Accardo, LPO, Dutoit 2536-376, TC 3336-376
    Arrangement for violin and piano—(Hasson, Brown) K53537, TCK453537
Perpetuela (Sonata Movimento Perpetuo)
    Accardo, LPO, Dutoit 2536-376, TC 3336-376

La Primavera
   Accardo, LPO, Dutoit 2530-900
Sonata con variazioni ('Sonata Militaire')
   Accardo, LPO, Dutoit 2536-376
Napoleon Sonata
   Accardo, LPO, Dutoit 2536-376, TC 3336-376
Variations, 'Le Streghe'
   Accardo, LPO, Dutoit 2530-714, TC 3300-714
   Arr. for violin and piano (Ricci, Persinger) ECS 585
Introduction and Variations on a theme from Paisiello's 'La bella molinara'
('Nel cor più non mi sento')
   Accardo, LPO, Dutoit 2707-107
   arr. for violin and piano – (Ricci, Persinger) ECS 585
La Campanella (arr. Kreisler)
   Oistrakh, Zertsalova UACL 10003
Cantabile (D)
   Terebesi, Prunnbauer AS 641300
   Perlman, Williams 76525, TC 40-67525
   Hasson, Brown K53537, TC K453537
   Oistrakh, Zertsalova UACL 10003
24 Caprices (solo violin)
   Ricci ECS 803, TC KSXC 2194
   Zukofsky VCS 10093-4
   Perlman ASD 3384, TC ASD 3384
   Accardo 2707-107
   Perlman SLS 832
   1-3, 5-9, 10, 17, 20, 24 (with pno accomp)
   Oistrakh, Zertsalova UACL 10003
   5, 13, Hasson K53537, TC 453537
   9, 24, Perlman SEOM 22
   24 (arr. for guitar)
   Williams 72728, TC 40-672728
   Williams 73745
   Williams 73784, TC 40-73784
18 Sonatas (Violin and guitar)
   1, 3, 4, 6 Terebesi, Prunnbauer AS6 41300
   1 Perlman, Williams 76525, TC 40-76525
   2, 5 Terebesi, Prunnbauer AS6 41936
Introduction and Variations on the theme from Rossini's 'Moses' ('Dal tuo
stellato soglio')
   Ricci, Persinger ECs 585
   Terebesi, Prunnbauer AS6 41995
   Oistrakh, Zertsalova UACL 10003
Grand Sonata (A) (Guitar and violin)
   Pasquier, Ghiglia CSD 3511
   Terebesi, Prunnbauer AS6 41300
   Perlman, Williams 76525, TC 40-76525
   Terebesi, Prunnbauer AS6 41936
Terzetto from Guitar Quartet No. 7
   Walker, Gesie, Roczek, Tachezi TV 343225
Introduction and Variations on a theme from Rossini's 'Tancredi' ('Di tanti
palpiti')
   Ricci, Persinger ECS 585
   Hasson, Brown K53537, TC K453537

163

Moto Perpetuo (C)
   Ricci, Persinger ECS 585
   St. Martin's Ac. Marriner TC 7317-034
   (Arr. for flute) Galway, Nat.PO, Gerdhardt LRLI-5127
   Oistrakh, Zertsalova UACL 1003
Romanz (Am)
   Scheit TV 34123S, TC KTVC 34123
Sonata for large Viola (Cm)
   Asciolla, LPO, Dutoit 2530-629
   Arad, Phil. Hungarica, Peters AW6-42007
   Koch, Luxemburg RO, Cao TV 34606S
Sonata (A) arr. for guitar
   Williams 72348, TC 40-72348
   Williams 73745
   Bream SB 6844
   Terebesi, Prunnbauer AS6 41300
Sonata (C) for solo violin
   Accardo 2707-107
6 Sonatas for violin and guitar (Op. 2)
   Terebesi, Prunnbauer AS6 41936
   No. 6 Terebesi, Prunnbauer AS6 41300
6 Sonatas for violin and guitar (Op. 3)
   Terebesi, Prunnbauer AS6 41995
   Bradley, Leeb GL 25095
   No. 6 Perlman, Williams 76525, TC 40-76525
   No. 6 (arr. violin and piano) Ricci, Persinger ECS 585
Tarantella (Am) (arr. for violin and guitar)
   Terebesi, Prunnbauer AS6 41995
Terzetto Concertante (D) (arr. from Guitar quartet No. 7)
   Walker, Geise, Tachezi TV 34322S
   Williams, Loveday, Fleming 73745
Vari•tions on 'God Save the King'
   Accardo 2707-107
   (Arr. for violin and piano) Ricci, Persinger ECS 585

Six
SELECT AIRS
from the most admired Works of
NICOLO PAGANINI
Performed by him at the Kings Theatre & Public Concerts.

namely.

March.

Monfrina.

Military Rondeau.

La Campanilla.

Rondeau.

and

The Witches Dance.

Arranged for the

Piano Forte,
BY
T. B. PHIPPS.

Pr. 3/

LONDON.

Published for the Author & Sold by Z. T. Purday 45. High Holborn.

Title page of a book containing airs played by Paganini at the King's Theatre

Sample of Paganini's text from the "Mastos Sonata Sentimentale" (above), and from the "Sonata Varsavia" (below), both for violin and orchestra

Paganini's "La Campanella" from the Rondo of the Second Violin Concerto, Opus 7

In 1831 the violinist-publisher, Nicholas Mori, asked Moscheles, a famous virtuoso pianist, to make some piano arrangements of Paganini's original tunes. Moscheles played them to Paganini while he was in London and Niccolo expressed his delight with them. The first volume, of which this is the cover page, was such a success that Mori published two more volumes. Paganini, who was by then (1832) experiencing a slump in his concert receipts, claimed that he had given permission for only one volume and sued both Mori and Moscheles for damages. After a long legal battle the matter was settled out of court but the famous pianist never forgave Paganini and became one of his severest critics.

Some Derivatives from Paganini –popular and serious

Drama

Paganini, an operetta with music by Franz Léhar based on the story of Paganini's 'love affair' with Princess Elise.

Film

The Magic Bow featuring Stewart Granger. Music arranged by Phil Green. Released, 1946

Orchestral items

Paganini Waltz by Dudley E. Bayford (pub. 1964).

Variations (Op. 26) by Boris Blacher, based on Caprice No. 24 (first performed in Frankfurt, 1951).

Suite by Michael Brussellmans, based on some of the 24 Caprices.

Variations for Orchestra by John Dankworth, on Caprice No. 24 (first performed 1975 and subsequently by John Dankworth and his quartet).

Variations by Benny Goodman (arr. Skip Martin) (pub. 1941).

Variations for 'cello and Rock Band by Andrew Lloyd Webber, on Caprice No. 24 (First performed 1977 at Symonton Festival. Recorded, in expanded version, 1978 – MCF 2824. Also available on tape).

Rhapsody on a Theme of Paganini for Piano and Orchestra (Op. 43) by Rachmaninoff, based on Caprice No. 24 (first performed 1934).

Paganini Samba by Wilson and Rogers.

Solo Instrumental items

Variations on a theme of Paganini for organ by G. Thalben Ball, based on Caprice No. 24 (pub. 1962).

Studies on a Theme of Paganini for piano by Brahms. Two sets of variations on Caprice No. 24 (pub. 1866).

Arrangement of the Brahms Studies, for guitar, by Eric Kershaw (pub. 1963).

Etudes d'Execution Transcendentales d'après Paganini for piano by Liszt, based on Caprice No. 24 (pub. 1840)

Variations on a Theme of Paganini for two pianos by Lutoslawski, based on Caprice No. 24 (pub. 1941).

Variations on the Caprice in A Minor (Op. 41) for three violins by Franco Mannino (pub. 1967 and later pub. as Op. 50 'for an orchestra of virtuosi').

Variations for solo violin by Manual Quiroga, based on Caprice No. 24 (pub. 1928).

Study for piano (Op. 3) by Schumann, a transcription of Caprice No. 24 (pub. 1832).

Grandes Variations Brilliantes on 'La Campanella' for piano duet by Carl Czerny.

Immediately after Paganini's début in Vienna, March 29th, 1828, the city was in a ferment of excitement about "this god of the violin", as one critic described him. Every shop displayed his portrait, every café-band played his tunes, every joke told in the street included a quip about him. He was even caricatured, appropriately perhaps, in the theatre. "Der Falsche Virtuose" or "Air on the G string", was a comic opera in two Acts, libretto by Karl Meisl, music by Frank Gläser (the "Gilbert and Sullivan" musical comedy team of the age), which had its first performance at the Carl Theatre on May 22nd. Although it had only twelve performances, it was extremely popular but Paganini left no record of having seen it. This is a reproduction of the cover and first page of the prompt copy now in the Austrian National Library, who kindly supplied it.

Six Concert Studies for piano (Op. 10) by Schumann, based on caprice No. 24 (pub. 1833).

Carnival for piano (Op. 9) by Schumann. No. 17 is called 'Paganini' (pub. 1834).

Variations for Clarinet and piano by James Walker, based on Caprice No. 24 (pub. 1977).

Songs

Mr. Paganini, you'll have to swing it by Sam Coslo (pub. 1936).

The Wonderful Paganini or 'London Fiddling Mad', words by W. T. Moncrieff.

Mr. Paganini, swing for Minnie by Lambert and Richardson (pub. 1938).

166

Sketch from a concert as Paganini played all E string passages in high positions of A

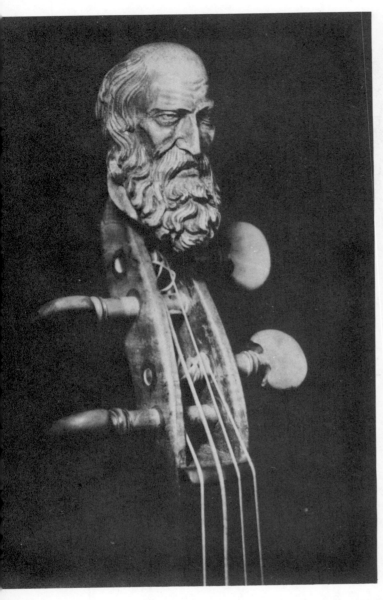

Violin ornamentations, inspired by Paganini

Index

Bold entries indicate illustrations

Tomb of Paganini

ILLUSTRATIONS ADDED FOR EXPANDED EDITION

In creating this expanded edition, more than fifty illustrations have been added as un-numbered pages at various places within the text. Following is a key to those insertions.

Theodore Roosevelt
  National Memorial Park
  Established April 25, 1947
  70,436 acres

Saguaro
  Established March 1, 1933
  79,084 acres

Sleeping Bear Dunes Natl. Lakeshore
  Authorized October 21, 1970
  71,068 acres

Sunset Crater
  Established May 26, 1930
  3,040 acres

Timpanogos Cave
  Established October 14, 1922
  250 acres

Upper Mississippi River
  Wildlife and Fish Refuge
  Established June 7, 1924
  194,940 acres
  32,985 in Minnesota
  87,987 in Wisconsin
  50,707 in Iowa
  23,261 in Illinois
  284 miles of river

White Sands
  Established January 18, 1933
  146,535 acres

National Wild and Scenic River
System
  Established October 2, 1968
  Original rivers:
    Eleven Point - 45 miles
    Feather (middle fork) - 108 miles
    Clearwater (middle fork) - 185 miles
      incl. Selway and Lochsa rivers
    Salmon (middle fork) - 104 miles
    Rio Grande - 52 miles
      incl. Red River
    Rogue - 84 miles
    Saint Croix - 185 miles
      incl. Namekagon River
    Wolf - 24 miles
  Added:
    Allagash - 92 miles

PHOTOGRAPHERS

The Editors of Country Beautiful wish to thank the following photographers for their contribution to this book:

Ansel Adams, Carmel, California

Thayne I. Andersen, Salt Lake City, Utah

Don C. Arns, Loveland, Colorado

Bureau of Sport Fisheries and Wildlife:R. L. Blott, J. S. Dixon, Luther C. Goldman, J. Malcolm Greany, E. R. Kalmbach, Eugene Kridler, David B. Marshall, Joseph Mazzoni, Rex Gary Schmidt, Leon C. Synder.

Cyr Agency, New Canaan, Connecticut: John Allen, Greene, F. G. Irwin, Richard Parker, Thrue-Yann.

Ted Czolowski, Vancouver, British Columbia

David Dale Dickey, Maryville, Tennessee

Michael Dunn, Tigard, Oregon

James Fain, Logan, Utah

Freelance Photographers Guild, New York, New York

Shelly Grossman, New York, New York

Robert Gunning, Seattle, Washington

Hildebrand Studio, Milwaukee, Wisconsin

Philip Hyde, Taylorsville, California

Doyle Kline, Santa Fe, New Mexico

Karl H. Maslowski, Cincinnati, Ohio

Steve and Dolores McCutcheon, Anchorage, Alaska

James J. McDonough, Jr., Las Vegas, Nevada

Wilford L. Miller, Bismarck, North Dakota

David Muench, Santa Barbara, California

Tom Myers, Sacramento, California

National Park Service:
  Bob Bergman, Jack Dermid, Youse Eliason, George A. Grant, John Kauffmann, William S. Keller, Fred E. Mang, Jr., Cecil W. Stoughton, Roger W. Toll, Volney J. Westley, M. Woodbridge Williams.

David C. Ochsner, Grand Canyon, Arizona

Vivian Pfleiderer, Sacramento, California

James W. Power, Seattle, Washington

H. Armstrong Roberts, Philadelphia, Pennsylvania

Bill Jack Rodgers, Los Alamos, New Mexico

Ken Short, Chicago, Illinois

Gordon S. Smith, East Harwich, Massachusetts

Werner Stoy, Honolulu, Hawaii

United States Forest Service

Utah Highway Department

William J. Weber, Leesburg, Florida

Stephen Guion Williams, Berwyn, Pennsylvania

Wisconsin Department of Natural Resources, Madison, Wisconsin

John V. Young, Los Alamos, New Mexico

APPENDIX

Agate Fossil Beds
Authorized June 5, 1965
3,051 acres

Apostle Islands National Lakeshore
Established September 26, 1970
42,826 acres

Aransas
Established December 31, 1937
54,829 acres

Arches
Established April 12, 1929
82,954 acres

Assateague Island National Seashore
Established September 21, 1965
39,630 acres

Badlands
Established January 25, 1939
243,508 acres

Biscayne
Established June 12, 1970
95,064 acres

National Bison Range
Established May 23, 1908
18,540 acres

Black Canyon of the Gunnison
Established March 2, 1933
13,667 acres

Buck Island Reef
Established December 28, 1961
850 acres

Cape Cod National Seashore
Established August 7, 1961
44,600 acres

Cape Hatteras National Seashore
Established January 12, 1953
28,500 acres

Cape Lookout National Seashore
Authorized March 10, 1966
24,500 acres

Capitol Reef
Established August 2, 1937
254,242 acres

Capulin Mountain
Established August 9, 1916
776 acres

Cedar Breaks
Established August 22, 1933
6,155 acres

Channel Islands
Established April 26, 1938
18,167 acres

Chincoteague
Established May 13, 1943
9,439 acres (part of Assateague
National Seashore)

Chiricahua
Established April 18, 1924
10,646 acres

Colorado
Established May 24, 1911
17,669 acres

Craters of the Moon
Established May 2, 1924
53,545 acres

Death Valley
Established February 11, 1933
1,907,760 acres

Desert National Wildlife Range
Established May 20, 1936
1,588,459 acres

Devils Postpile
Established July 6, 1911
798 acres

Devils Tower
Established September 24, 1906
1,347 acres

Dinosaur
Established October 4, 1915
206,663 acres

Fire Island National Seashore
Authorized September 11, 1964
19,311 acres

Florissant Fossil Beds
Authorized August 20, 1969
5,992 acres

Glacier Bay
Established February 26, 1925
2,803,840 acres

Grand Canyon
Established December 22, 1932
198,280 acres

Great Sand Dunes
Established March 17, 1932
36,740 acres

Gulf Islands National Seashore
Authorized January 8, 1971
163,200 acres

Hawaiian Islands
Established February 3, 1909
1,765 acres

Ice Age National Scientific Reserve
Established May 29,1971
32,500 acres

Indiana Dunes National Lakeshore
Authorized November 5, 1966
8,721 acres

Jewel Cave
Established February 7, 1908
1,275 acres

Joshua Tree
Established August 10, 1936
558,184 acres

Katmai
Established September 24, 1918
2,792,137 acres

Kodiak
Established August 19, 1941
1,815,000 acres

Lava Beds
Established November 21, 1925
46,239 acres

Lehman Caves
Established January 24, 1922
640 acres

Loxahatchee
Established June 8, 1951
145,635 acres

Marble Canyon
Established January 20, 1969
32,665 acres

Monomoy
Established June 1, 1944
2,698 acres

Moosehorn
Established July 1, 1937
22,666 acres

Muir Woods
Established January 9, 1908
503 acres

Natural Bridges
Established April 16, 1908
7,600 acres

Okefenokee
Established March 30, 1937
368,446 acres

Oregon Caves
Established July 12, 1909
480 acres

Organ Pipe Cactus
Established April 13, 1937
330,874 acres

Ozark National Scenic Riverways
Established August 27, 1964
72,101 acres; 140 miles of rivers

Padre Island National Seashore
Authorized September 28, 1962
133,918 acres

Pea Island
Established April 8, 1938
5,915 acres (part of Cape Hatteras
National Seashore)

Pictured Rocks National Lakeshore
Established October 15, 1966
67,000 acres

Pinnacles
Established January 16, 1908
14,498 acres

Point Reyes National Seashore
Established September 13, 1962
64,546 acres

Rainbow Bridge
Established May 30, 1910
160 acres